The
Message

The
Message

100 LIFE LESSONS
FROM HIP-HOP'S
GREATEST SONGS

Felicia Pride

THUNDER'S MOUTH PRESS • NEW YORK

THE MESSAGE:
100 Life Lessons from Hip-Hop's Greatest Songs

Published by
Thunder's Mouth Press

AVALON

Copyright © 2007 by Felicia Pride

First Printing October 2007

Thunder's Mouth Press books are available at special discounts for bulk purchases in the United States by corporations, institutions, and other organizations. For more information, please contact the Special Markets Department at the Perseus Books Group, 2300 Chestnut Street , Suite 200, Philadelphia, PA 19103, or call (800) 255-1514, or e-mail special.markets@perseusbooks.com

Library of Congress Cataloging-in-Publication Data is available.

ISBN-10: 1-56858-335-4
ISBN-13: 978-1-56858-335-8

BOOK DESIGN BY PAULINE NEUWIRTH, NEUWIRTH & ASSOCIATES, INC.

Printed in the United States of America
www.perseusbooks.com

To my three ladies, thanks for loving all of me.
To Felix, 'nuff said.

Contents

PART TWO: *Cashmere Thoughts*

PART THREE: *Politics as Usual*

PART FOUR: *Love's Gonna Get cha*

PART FIVE: *Life Is What You Make It*

PART SIX: H-U-S-T-L-E

Acknowledgments

THERE HAVE BEEN so many people who have helped me along this journey. I've been blessed to have some really supportive people cross my path. Please forgive me if I fail to mention you here, but know that my heart thanks you.

First, I must thank God. If you weren't moving through me, there wouldn't be a book. When I didn't think I could do this, you thought otherwise.

Special thanks to Adrienne Ingrum, my agent and mentor. I still remember the day we had tea and talked about what would become this book. Isn't it amazing how things come together? Thanks for always being available to chat and letting me know that everything will be okay.

Thanks to my editor, Anita Diggs. You're on my "Down from Day One" list! Thanks so much for your support and for giving *The Message* a home. Thanks to the entire staff at Thunder's Mouth Press for helping me to produce such a great project.

Thanks to Momma for life. How can I truly thank you? Thanks for listening to me vent. Thanks for reading my work and giving me feedback.

Thanks for loving me at first sight. And thanks to Fellina, my second half. You've always supported me. I can't wait to read your manuscript! Thanks, Ms. Brynn, for sharing your room with me. And thanks for letting me see what I was like when I was younger. Thanks, Felix, for your supportive words. I'm going to put you to work to help me sell this book! To Mr. Gordon, thanks for making my mother happy. You don't know how important that is to me.

To José, you are a Ghostface verse over a Premo beat. For the past few years you've been my rock. Thanks for listening to the telenovella that's My Life. Thanks for being there when others weren't. Thanks for telling me I could do this. Thanks for being you. To my girl Sai, my DJ, my cheerleader. We never did tour with BBD, but we're still taking over! Thanks for telling everyone how great I am. To my homies—Erin W., Dominique B., Calcie C., Terrance B., Stacia B., Tawny P., David D. (can't wait to ghostwrite your book), and Tammy H.—thanks for kicking it with me.

Thanks to all the wordsmiths whom I've had the pleasure to meet and work with—Mark Anthony Neal (your support of my work has meant so much), Kalisha Buckhanon, Kim McLarin, Sofía Quintero, Brian Peterson, Kwame Alexander, Orlando Lima, Renee Flagler, Miles Marshall Lewis, Michael Gonzales, Lynne D. Johnson, Debbie Rigaud, Karen Valentin, Lawrence Ross, Tina McElroy Ansa, and Ken Gibbs. Thanks to Joan Morgan, your encouraging words went a long way. Thanks to the hip-hoppers and grinders who spared a few minutes for me—Bobbito Garcia, Little Brother, Ed O.G., Akrobatik, Monie Love, and Pharoahe Monch. Special thanks to the publishing and literary folks who've supported me—Linda Duggins, Malaika Adero, Calvin Reid, Charles Harris, Barbara Summers, Carol Mackey, Melody Guy, Kelli Martin, Krishan Trotman, Doug Seibold, Johnny Temple, Johanna Ingalls, Lisa Kaufman, Stacey Barney, Rakia Clark, Clarence Haynes, Clarence Reynolds, Susan McHenry, Ken Smikle, Karen Thomas, Mondella Jones, Regina Brooks, Sherrie Young, Lynette Velasco, John McGregor, Ron Kavanaugh, Patrick Oliver, Troy Johnson, Sherri Sonnier, and Jill Petty. Special thanks to Juris Jurjevics for everything! I'm so glad I had the opportunity to take your publishing class. Thanks to Jeffrey Seglin for all your support at Emerson. Your column writing class came in handy while I wrote this book. Thanks to Bret McCabe at the Baltimore *City Paper* for telling me that my voice was one that deserved to be heard. I have to thank Ohhla.com. The Web site was indispensable to me in writing this book.

Thanks to all of my family in Baltimore. Special thanks to Symone, Aunt Bert, Uncle Preston, Aunt Marge, Aunt Margie, Aunt Marion, Cousin Maxine, Uncle Jerome and Aunt Maggie, Aunt Annie and the Kiser Clan, Aunt Laura, Alexis, Aunt Sondra, Aunt Barbara, and Aunt Mildred. To Uncle Ishmael, you haunt my thoughts. I can't wait to write your story.

And lastly, thanks to hip-hop for giving me a reason to write.

Introduction

I **WAS RIDING** on the train one day traveling from Brooklyn into Manhattan. Broke. Squished between two passengers. Couldn't sit back in the seat. I was in that pensive mode, where I worked hard to shut out everything around me, including the passengers I was squeezed between, the tourists snapping photos of the inside of a subway car, and the irritating announcer who kept telling me to say something if I see something. I was contemplating my life, my future, and the suffocating bedroom that I was occupying in Crown Heights because it was all that I could afford. I was thinking about leaving my comfortable, average-wage job and devoting my time to Me, Inc. I wanted to take the steps toward professional freedom where I decided what time I rose in the morning and which projects deserved my attention.

It didn't help matters that the fabulous life I was supposed to live in New York was a perpetual cycle of empty bank accounts, lofty ambitions that I couldn't seem to achieve (like living without a roommate), and teases from my passion. Allow me to cut to the chase: I was unhappy.

So as I sat on the train—the meat in an uncomfortable sandwich, trying to think in the midst of chaos—my iPod provided the sanity I needed to get me through my adventures in the land of Postgraduationunhappilyever-after. A Tribe Called Quest's classic hip-hop contribution, *The Low End Theory*, blared through my headphones. I heard the music but knew the album so well that I wasn't really listening. That is, until Phife Dawg, in one eloquent rhyme, captured how I was living. On "Buggin' Out," he says simply and poignantly, "Riding on the train with no dough, sucks." If I could have, I would have jumped up with a loud "Amen" like I was in church. (I couldn't even raise my arms, it was that tight between my fellow passengers.) I played the line again. Again. And again. I didn't want to ride the train broke anymore. How could I change my situation?

I called my boy to tell him my new mantra. This is what I do. Adopt a hip-hop rhyme and claim it as a guiding life principle. I remember describing to him in great detail my epiphany moment. "I need to take control of my life," I told him. "I'm tired of riding the train broke." Yep, my mission to become an independent (read *quit my job and work for Me, Myself, and I*) was partly prompted by a hip-hop lyric. I'd be rich or at least able to afford a one-bedroom apartment in Manhattan if I had a nickel for each time I heard a rhyme that's written for me. One that speaks directly to me, like the MC is peering into my life at that moment and creating a theme song to accompany it.

Here's another time it happened. I'm listening to Common's *Be* on the way to a meeting with a book publishing veteran. I had recently left my job (partly thanks to Phife) to helm Me, Inc., and was networking like a PC.

I heard the album on a few thousand occasions, but this time, on "They Say," when the sexy-brained MC rhymed "writin' for my life 'cause I'm scared of a day job" I paused on the stairs to the subway, shook my head, did a quick rewind, and smiled. Common articulated exactly what I was feeling. Hip-hop never ceased to amaze me.

Over tea, the publishing veteran and I talked casually about the book industry and our freelance work. We vibed, and for the first time, I uttered an amorphous idea for a book. This is how I loosely explained the concept:

> *In my day-to-day, I quote hip-hop lyrics as life-defining mantras. I recall lines and ideas from songs as a way to explain this crazy existence. On the way over here, I was listening to Common and he spit a line that explained exactly how I feel. There are tons of rhymes like this that can, in an instant, describe my ambitions, dreams, and my life. I want to write a book that's motivational in nature and explores an aspect of hip-hop lifestyle that's rarely covered. There's a hip-hop song that can match any one of my moods, encapsulate my rage, put a smile on my face, make me thankful for my mother, and make me repent to God. I want to write a book that explains how I use hip-hop every day when I walk out of my house. I know I'm not the only one. This is what hip-hoppers do.*

And that's what I set out to do.

I won't bore you with a nostalgic and dreamy account of how I first fell in love with hip-hop. To be honest, I don't remember. Trying to pinpoint a specific moment would be the equivalent of recalling the first time I fell in love with myself. I wasn't at a basement party somewhere, heard a tight rhyme, and *bam!* Hip-Hop cupid shot me in the ear. It was a much more fluid and organic process.

What I do know is that I was born in 1979. Thus, I don't know a world without hip-hop. I was born into "Rapper's Delight," which makes my experience quite different from the scores of hip-hoppers who've previously written books about the culture. Many of them remember rocking at block parties and relish their stirring in-person memories of hip-hop's architects like Grandmaster Flash, Afrika Bambaataa, Melle Mel, Kool Herc, DJ Hollywood, Funky 4 + 1, and the Cold Crush Brothers engaging in pristine artistic expression. Their stories make me wish that I, too, had witnessed the birth of a nation.

I'm like the middle child within the hip-hop generation. Like my elders, hip-hoppers born before the mid '70s, I cringe at the gratuitous money-hungry, violent, misogynistic, and lackluster turn of some of the music. And unlike my younger siblings, '80s and '90s babies, I do remember the days when the radio played fun rap, Afrocentric rap, gutter rap, jazzy rap, and educational rap all in one sixty-minute segment. I remember when you had to have skills to be put on as an MC. Period.

Although I can't always get with the Lil' rappers who my younger siblings consider the greatest, I don't necessarily play the purist role that some of my elders assume. I do believe that banging hip-hop music has been produced after 1996. Many of my elders have given up on hip-hop because the culture they knew—the culture they rocked to as they came of age—is unrecognizable. Many of them have moved on. They are over hip-hop.

I haven't reached that point yet—that place of disillusionment, frustration, and abandonment. This may well be generational, but I think it has more to do with the fact that I carefully select aspects of hip-hop that align with my life. My siblings, young and old, want to define what hip-hop should be. Often, I also find myself engaging in this territorial activity. We've forgotten that hip-hop, at its core, is creative self-expression. It only makes sense that the individual defines his or her own place within it. Accordingly, I've carved a space that I affectionately call MyHipHop.

Things have changed in hip-hop. I won't delve heavily into the obvious. Rap music has been corporatized and doesn't answer to the streets but to phat bottom lines. These days rappers rarely move crowds; they move units to the highest bidders. Let me put it another way. Back in the day, I knew I couldn't rhyme. I had no flow. But I'll bet if I bought a two-piece from Victoria's Secret and sported it as an outfit, I, too, could get a record deal. Hip-Hop has changed.

MyHipHop, however, is alive and kicking snares. Thriving. I don't worry about being trendy with MyHipHop. I throw on *The Very Best of Big Daddy Kane* and rock to "Young, Gifted and Black" like it was released yesterday. The playlist of MyHipHop is a mixture of goodies that never get old, dope mainstream MCs, and a posse of indie cats who rock, rock on. MyHipHop doesn't go out of style and isn't dictated by Universal Music Group or Clear Channel. MyHipHop is found in universities and on the blocks of Your City. MyHipHop develops educational curriculums to teach the culture as a tool of empowerment. MyHipHop congregates young people for antiwar demonstrations. MyHipHop is artistic and creative. MyHipHop elevates, challenges, and excites me. MyHipHop does not stop.

It's safe to say that every writer who is also a hip-hop head, or better yet every hip-hop head who is also a writer, has a gnawing feeling to write a book about the culture. If we were artists, we would drop an album; instead, we embrace the charge to express ourselves and our love for the culture through a nail-biting process of producing a hip-hop manuscript. That ain't easy. To give justice to a sprawling culture, insert yourself into the equation, reconcile any politics (i.e., I'm pro-woman and hip-hop, how do I maintain both?), and not repeat what's already been done is a monumental task.

Despite the personal war that takes place when one writes a book, many do it. And many hip-hoppers have done it. I think I own nearly every one of these important texts. Some have been academic in nature, like *That's the Joint!: The Hip-Hop Studies Reader* edited by Mark Anthony Neal and Murray Forman. Others have been historical accounts that trace the roots of the culture like the very necessary *Can't*

Stop Won't Stop: A History of the Hip-Hop Generation by Jeff Chang, a few have looked at artistic aesthetics like William Jelani Cobb's *To the Break of Dawn: A Freestyle on the Hip-Hop Aesthetic*, a handful are memoirs with hip-hop backdrops like *Scars of the Soul Are Why Kids Wear Bandages When They Don't Have Bruises* by Miles Marshall Lewis, and still others have been sociopolitical analyses like Yvonne Bynoe's *Stand and Deliver: Political Activism, Leadership, and Hip Hop Culture.*

Like many of these books, *The Message* is my tribute to a culture that plays a pivotal role in my life—the same culture that showed me early on that I deserved to write about how I feel and that what I scribed was valid and important. Additionally, I wanted to expose the rays of light that hip-hop shines into so many of our lives. I wanted to revisit, even in the midst of hip-hop's internal and external conflicts, why we love the culture so: it speaks to us.

In *The Message* I play a favorite role of hip-hoppers, that of interpreter. Oh, we love to sit around and decipher what MCs have said, are trying to say, or didn't say but we know they meant to. Funny enough, when I arrived at Emerson College's graduate writing program, I had years of experience in literary analysis and didn't realize it. I had been deconstructing themes and narratives since *The Great Adventures of Slick Rick*. Using that skill, what I've attempted to do in this book is extract motivational mantras, life lessons, and positive principles from hip-hop songs where I've found meaning. I explore themes of individuality, love, politics, spirituality, and passion and, when appropriate, connect them to even larger life ideas.

It must be said that these interpretations are based on my opinions and perspectives. You know how it is when you debate with someone about the merits of Biggie's lyricism versus that of 2Pac's—there's always some disagreement, but that doesn't mean that one opinion is more valid than another. Additionally, my interpretation may be different from the artist's intention. But that's the beauty of art. It exposes itself to multiple perspectives.

Although I marvel at the artistic expressions of our greatest MCs, this book isn't about their skills. *The Message* is really about us. When I say "us" or "we" throughout the book, I'm referring to the hip-hop generation, my siblings, young and old. One hundred times I answer the question, *What is the message, and how can we use it in our own lives?*

That takes us to the title of this book, which is derived from the 1982 song performed by Grandmaster Flash and The Furious Five. Originally written by Ed "Duke Bootee" Fletcher with Melle Mel, the song is still one of the most stirring hip-hop narratives. It's conscious without being didactic. An early example of what hip-hop can be: aware, successful, and influential. A lasting example of what we can be.

Hip-hop fans are a passionate bunch. So allow me to make the following disclaimer: *The Message* includes *some* of the greatest hip-hop songs. This is by no means a Top 100 list, nor does the book attempt to include *all* of hip-hop's greatest songs. I wouldn't wish that task on anyone. This is purely a sampling. Selecting only one hundred songs wasn't easy like Sunday mornings. There were many songs and artists I wanted to include (shout-out to Black Moon) but couldn't fit in this installment.

The selection process was calculating, arbitrary, and self-absorbed. I chose no-brainers like Public Enemy's "Don't Believe the Hype," seemingly unusual ones like Wu-Tang Clan's "Tearz," and songs close to my heart like Pharcyde's "Passing Me By."

During this very difficult process, I attended a party where the one and only D-Nice was on the wheels. He effortlessly mixed the old with the new, the classic with the obscure. My intent was to make the song collection in *The Message* just as eclectic and meaningful. I've included indie artists like Akrobatik; the usual suspects like Jigga, Nas, and Biggie; the forgotten like Souls of Mischief, although they're still rocking independently; and the architects like Bambaataa, Kane, and Rakim. If you dig for at least one of the included songs after reading this book, I've accomplished a small part of my goal.

"I'm a movement by myself, but I'm a force when we're together."
—From "Make Me Better" by Fabolous

My larger goal revolved around championing the "I" in hip-hop so that we can build the "we." Corny? Maybe. I'm in that weird place in my adulthood where I concentrate on crafting a life that means something. I want to spend the majority of my days with a smile on my face. I want to accomplish all of my goals and then some. For these reasons, I've sought motivational resources that could help in my emotional, mental, physical, and psychological elevation. In this pursuit of happiness, I realized that much of the wisdom that I craved can be found in my favorite hip-hop songs. What I also realized is that these gems weren't really collected anywhere, unless you count playlists in my iPod. So I did what hip-hoppers do—I created one. A collection of life lessons culled with you and me in mind. I'm not a preacher, guru, or a licensed psychologist with my own television show. I'm a black chick, a hip-hop head who doesn't want to ride the train broke. Who's with me?

Recently hip-hop has been the center of debate (this is nothing new) because of its increased participation in misogynistic, homophobic, and violent behavior. There's this misinformed argument that hip-hop, a form of creative expression that has transformed into a lifestyle, is to blame. Hip-hop's issues don't play out in us. Our issues play out in hip-hop. There's nothing inherently bad in hip-hop. Hip-hop doesn't call women b$tches, individuals do. Hip-hop doesn't sell subpar music, individuals and corporations do. With a little deductive reasoning in place, this is what I came up with: *if we are hip-hop and hip-hop is messed up, perhaps we need to get ourselves together.*

If we wait on hip-hop to propel a mass sociopolitical movement or change our lives, we may be waiting longer than the day when men become equipped to bear children. Hip-hop can be a positive muse for our actions, but it cannot be an activator. This book is about searching for the power within and using motivational aspects of hip-hop music to help us successfully maneuver our worlds.

Another disclaimer: I'm not interested in propelling MCs into positions of gurus and revering them as such (could you picture Jay-Z in a

Buddhist robe?). I am examining them as artists whose work offers glimpses into our own lives.

To know that I—little ol' me, who struggles when lifting heavy boxes—can affect monumental change in my own life and control my thoughts, attitudes, and perspectives is the most potent form of empowerment that I've come across. Many of us are victims of circumstance, but I ask the question, *How can we transform our realities just as brown and black kids did in the South Bronx and beyond?*

This book is about hip-hop. This book is not about hip-hop. This book is about choice—the multitude of choices we have but sometimes don't recognize. The choices we make in life and how they drive or stagnate us. There's a need for us to be honest about our issues and the weight of the baggage that we're lugging. It's my hope that this book will help us to identify and remove obstructions on our path to being the best us we can be. In doing so I'm sure a wave of change will flow through all of hip-hop.

The lessons in this book are ones that I've learned, am still grappling with, and that I needed to write so that I could bring them into existence into my own life. My hope is that one, many, or all of the lessons in this book will prompt change in your life as well, whether you're motivated to embrace your passion, seek love, live an abundant life, transform your community, or simply keep on keepin' on.

We can learn from hip-hop, which really means that we can learn from one another. And collectively, we can live the lives for which we are built.

*Doin'
Me*

PART ONE

1. Express Yourself

ARTIST: N.W.A.
ALBUM: STRAIGHT OUTTA COMPTON (1988)

MY LINGUAL AFFAIR with wordplay (that sounds so deliciously dirty) began as a one-night stand with hip-hop music that morphed into a relationship I never expected. When I was younger I was infatuated by the witty and often complex rhymes of wordsmiths like Big Daddy Kane and Slick Rick. In a single-subject notebook I would write down the lyrics to the dopest songs and practice the rhymes in the mirror. My fist was my mic. Without realizing it, I was developing a reverence for words. Meanwhile, in school, my teachers praised my writing. Coincidence? This is why I write.

N.W.A.'s "Express Yourself" is what happens when "gangstas" leave the drugs, violence, and profanity at home and bring themselves, intellect intact, into the studio booth. A young Dr. Dre, an original member of the Compton Crew that popularized an entire subgenre of rap music, comes from behind the production boards to tell the world that when you combine "a subject and a predicate" (a gangsta who knows his grammar) and add a tight rhythm, the result might "make you think."

When N.W.A. bumrushed hip-hop, I was miles away from Compton, not only in distance as a Jerzee girl, but also in environment. I had no clue what a '64 was but deduced it was some type of car and couldn't tell you what to do with a twelve gauge. All I knew was that those homies looked like my kin with Jheri curls and I, too, wanted to express myself using my "full capabilities."

Hip-hop not only gave voice to the voiceless but for this little brown girl, and I didn't know it then, the music was also an early introduction to a new personal narrative—the type that wasn't validated by my school studies; stories that dripped from the mouths of kids who weren't old, white, or dead. Compton cats, Brooklyn babies, and Bronx brothers were writing from their own perspective. People around the country were listening. Their words, thoughts, and ideas mattered. This was powerful to a little brown girl. This was powerful to many brown boys and girls.

So I figured if cats like N.W.A. and lyricists like Kane and Rick could command attention through mastery of their wordplay, I could, too. I immersed myself into the expressions of hip-hop's poets who were writing their lives. My personal voice began to develop.

Naturally, the first platform I sought to disseminate my voice was rapping. Had no flow. Tried to write rhymes and poetry. Was no Lauryn Hill. Would embarrass Nikki Giovanni. Began writing. Began writing about hip-hop music. Began writing about myself. Began writing about hip-hop culture. Continued writing about myself. Began writing books. Still write about myself. I have a story to tell. And people are reading it.

We all harbor a need to express ourselves whether it's through rhyming, writing, speaking, other artistic platforms, or through the life we lead. Many times, however, we convince ourselves, or allow others to do it for us, that the story we have to tell isn't important. We suffocate our inner expression and allow others to speak for us. Once we realize that our perspectives and experiences are worthy to be released to the world, it is very necessary for us to stand up and be seen, be heard, be read. Be understood.

Hip-hop helped to embolden me with a confidence to write from my vantage point with the same audacity exuded by N.W.A. in the opening scenes of the "Express Yourself" video as they rip through a full-size paper sign that reads "I Have A Dream." I've been opened up to write my truth, uniquely, and in my voice. Black-Female-Hip-hop. I insert myself into public conversation. I found my mic. And I continue to rip it.

This is why I write.

2. *The Meaning of the Name*

ARTIST: GANG STARR
ALBUM: STEP IN THE ARENA (1991)

ALLOW ME TO introduce Negra, my alter ego. When I'm too shy, nervous, or flat-out scared, I let her take over. She's fearless, daring, outspoken, and confident. She's smart as hell and knows how to work a room. She's the one who speaks in front of large groups with incredible poise and intellect. Negra approaches strangers and sparks conversation. If a dude with engaging eyes and a nice smile is available, she may ask for his number.

I picked up the handle one day in my college Spanish class when I learned that the word "*negra*" loosely translates into "black woman." That described me. I liked the way it rolled off my tongue. Over the years, I've also learned that *negra* can mean "unfortunate" and "angry." Word? Some people assume that I suffer from both of these definitions. So, the name stuck, and I did what hip-hoppers do: remixed it and made it my own.

In "The Meaning of the Name," Guru, one-half of the seminal hip-hop duo Gang Starr, breaks down the definition and positive symbolism behind the group's name, a moniker that Keith Elam (Guru) and

Christopher Martin (DJ Premier) created to represent their crew's (gang) power (starr). Using one word, Guru summarizes that the group's name is synonymous with "mastermind." It's through Gang Starr that Keith transformed into Guru, which has been said to also mean "Gifted Unlimited Rhymes Universal," and Guru became "free to bust rhymes sporadically." The power in the name.

Hip-hoppers have always assumed unusual aliases. A survey of the members of the Wu-Tang Clan—from Ol' Dirty Bastard to Ghost-face Killah—offers more than enough wild examples. And many of us have taken renaming to another level by also adopting additional personas.

When Eminem was trying to distinguish his hip-hop self in a black-dominated world, Slim Shady emerged—the insane, sickly flowed alter ego through which Eminem, aka Marshall Mathers, found a way to be heard and to be crazy. Likewise, I always wondered how Beyoncé could be bashful in interviews, but on stage become a rump-shaking, fearless diva. Then I learned about Sasha, her alternative self. It all made sense.

There's Shawn Carter the corporate head and Jay-Z the hustler. You can lose count of all the names and personas that Jigga has assumed over the years. Writer and hip-hop thinker Mark Anthony Neal notes that the "multiple persona" is common in hip-hop because we need to be "fluid in the various publics" in which many of us operate.

I first developed my alter ego specifically for that reason: to maneuver in the many different environments where I function. One day I'm in an office with corporate bigwigs, the next day with my students in the

South Bronx, the next on panels discussing literature or conversing with graduate school classmates, and then with my peoples in Baltimore.

Negra helps me maintain my flexibility and fearlessness. Some guzzle down a pint of Henny to release their inhibitions. I don't have the stomach or the pockets for all that. When it comes to overcoming the timidity that blocks us from handling our business, conjuring up our more confident side and attaching a name to it makes dollars and sense.

This isn't about being someone you're not. Representing Me, Myself, and I is still priority number one. This is about embracing our multiple selves—the Me, the Myself, and the I—and tapping into those reserves for the confidence, power, and sanity needed to accomplish our dreams. With that said, I want to take this time to thank Negra for helping me write this book. You a wild girl!

3. *Me Myself and I*

ARTIST: DE LA SOUL
ALBUM: 3 FEET HIGH AND RISING (1989)

"I'M REAL," **OR** the variant "Because I keep it real," has become a hip-hop household response to any question.

"Why do you mimic the lifestyle of a drug dealer?"

"Because I keep it real."

"Why don't you take care of your children?"

"Because I keep it real."

"Why did you put ketchup on your pizza?

"Because I keep it real."

"I'm real" has been so overused that its meaning is borderline null.

If you have to relentlessly boast that you're real until folks tune you out, chances are, you're no longer convincing others. You've run out of clever explanations, you're trying to believe your own tales that are taller than LeBron James, or most likely, you're avoiding the truth.

Let's face it, in the celebfest, pseudo-reality world we live in, it is much easier to sell an image, because representing the true you implies that (1) you're comfortable in your skin and many of us aren't; (2) you're not concerned with how people will receive the fullness of you; and

(3) you truly know who you are and accept that person, both the good and the bad. Profiling, fronting, and projecting are all much easier.

In "Me Myself and I," Posdnuos, Trugoy, and Mase, the former Native Tongues trio from Long Island, drop a blatant demand to the masses to let them be themselves. Between their offbeat styles; wide-ranging musical influences; intellectual, over-your-head rhymes; nongangster posturing; and D.A.I.S.Y. movement (which meant "da inner sound y'all"), De La were painted as psychedelic flower children after the release of their debut, *3 Feet High and Rising*. The need to recapture their identity was probably the motivation behind the title of their following album, *De La Soul Is Dead*.

This gap between "keeping it real" and actually being real is becoming so wide that at times we're liable to fall in as we try to decipher which is which and who is who. I remember dating a guy, an aspiring rapper, who any time he got around other people (especially his boys), his voice and speech changed, went from high-pitched to low and dark. He altered his stance; he walked slower and with a more defined bop. He exaggerated everything he was and wasn't doing.

At first his role-playing didn't bother me, until it became confusing. Which dude was I dating? He became this exaggerated hood character to enhance his street credibility. He allowed other people to decide who he should be—a shallow thug stereotype—when in fact the brother had levels.

Not only is it simpler to sell an image of ourselves, but it's also easier for others to digest a box-friendly stick figure instead of a fully diverse persona that many of us embody.

As a society, we like labels, boxes, and other ways to confine and categorize. We prejudge folks on various characteristics before they even open their mouths. Hair: you must light incense, meditate, and be peace-loving if you rock a natural style. Background: you must be ghetto if you grew up in the inner city. Musical tastes: you must want to be white if you listen to punk rock. There's always a level of disappointment for outsiders when we don't live up to misconceptions. Even if you're comfortable in your skin, and know exactly who you are, others aggressively attempt to promote their own idea of who you should be.

Defending our identity is a difficult but necessary fight, one that De La took seriously. We shouldn't spend our nights worrying about how others view us, but it is worthwhile to prevent any infringements on our character.

That's why I appreciate the people in my life who allow me to be me, myself, and I. They don't need me to fulfill a fantastical image. They also allow me to exercise my right to reinvent myself, to change, and to grow. I've spent too much time, the bulk of my twenties, trying to understand and learn who I am to allow my beautifully complex person to be diminished to a cardboard cutout.

Trust, it can be lonely on Do You Boulevard. Everyone's chilling at the corner of Popular Street, and you're solo—just you, yourself, and lots of space. But I believe that a city (read *society*) is built when folks pave their own streets.

Come check me around the way at This Is Me Avenue.

4. *Not Enough*

ARTIST: LITTLE BROTHER, FEATURING DARIEN BROCKINGTON
ALBUM: THE MINSTREL SHOW (2005)

OVER THE YEARS, I've been told that I'm not _____ enough. Fill in the blank with a variety of words, including *hardworking*, *sexy*, *freaky*, *nice*, *mean*, *outspoken*, *attractive*, *motherly*, and *phat* (when I was twelve, a fifteen-year-old dude from around my cousin's way used my flat curves as an explanation of why he didn't like me).

I've also been accused of being too _____. Again, fill in the blanks with *hardworking*, *nice*, *mean*, *outspoken*, *sensitive*, *smart*, *ambitious*, *independent*, and *giving*. Notice that some of the same words are on both lists. Bottom line: no matter what I do, it's like the world around me suffers from a warped Goldilocks complex where I'm either too much or not enough. Never just right.

Of course, there's a song that airs my vexation. According to Phonte of Little Brother, a group that represents for everyday cats, the concept behind "Not Enough" evolved after an ill-received homecoming performance at their alma mater, North Carolina Central University. Instead of supporting a group from their neck of the woods, the audience stared at them, waiting for them to blow up. The experience turned into a song with "dope beats" and "dope rhymes" and the defining question, "What more do y'all want?"

The song isn't just about satisfying fickle rap fans, Phonte told me.

"When I wrote the hook, I wasn't just thinking about the hip-hop side of things," he said. "I was thinking about life in general."

Why are people so hard to please?

I once had a girlfriend joke with me that she can cook, clean, submit, fry chicken Butterball-naked, serve it to her man, allow him to watch the game, and still he wouldn't be satisfied. Instead, the chicken would be too salty. Granted she's exaggerating, but I get her point. I've found myself trying to overcompensate in relationships, in my career, and in my day-to-day, with the mind-set that the more I give, the more I should get back. Only to be left with a Coke and no smile.

Maybe as human beings we're just spoiled. Maybe some universal gene makes us feel entitled to everything and then some. Maybe it's just a societal ill (capitalism?) that makes us insatiable. Maybe we don't know what we really want, so we keep asking for more.

Unfortunately, the dump truck of frustration piles it on thick, and the odor that wafts through the air smells like surrender. We're urged to stop blessing the ungrateful, undeserving masses with our talent. To stop loving because our affection is never sufficient. To simply stop. Quitting is always an easy option, but rarely a solution. The fact is blatant: *we will never be able to satisfy everyone.* The pursuit of this lofty dream is a full-time job with no benefits, just negative performance reviews. All we can do is do what we do, and do it the best way we know how.

I don't play Mad Libs with folks anymore. I fill in my own blanks. On good days, I'm __damn__ good, and on bad days, I'm __damn__ good. Get used to me.

5. *What They Do*

ARTIST: THE ROOTS, FEATURING RAPHAEL SAADIQ
ALBUM: ILLADELPH HALFLIFE (1996)

I ALWAYS THOUGHT that the parental retort "Would you jump off a ten-story building if your friends did it?" was quite silly. Of course the answer is no, unless you have a death wish or enjoy the extreme sport of BASE jumping.

So without any real fear that I might plunge to my death, I've followed the crowd from time to time. I remember having an adolescent fit when my mother told me she wouldn't buy me a pair of Skidz pants because they "looked like pajamas that she could sew herself." How would I look if all my classmates rocked Skidz and I wore handmade flannel wannabes?

Truth is, I didn't really like the pants. They were funny-looking. But my mother didn't have to know that. At that age, assimilating was the easiest weapon against getting cracked on. That was then, and now I realize that too much assimilation isn't always a good thing. It's actually grown folks' way of being uncreative and lazy. Trends are easier to embrace. Even in adulthood, there's an absent desire to assert one's individuality.

The Roots aren't lazy. The Philly-representing group popularized the hip-hop band, with in-house keyboardist, drummer, and guitarist—something I hadn't really seen before they sprouted onto the scene. In the mid '90s "What They Do" smoothly attacked trends in rap music such as the no skillz, frontin' one-dimensional rapper (will he ever go away?). To accompany the song's contempt, the Roots also produced a witty parody of the average rap video that could have been a segment on *Chappelle's Show*. The scenes of rented mansions, aimless car drives to nowhere, bikinied girls dancing around the pool with booties rocking precisely to the beat, and crew champagne popping, continue to be mainstays in today's rap videos. Visuals that seem as ridiculous as those overpriced pajama pants I craved.

The Roots' advice to counteract wackness by association, sung by the multitalented Raphael Saadiq, was straight to the point, "never do . . . what they do."

There's always that potential pitfall of paying too much attention to "what they do" and not to what we can do differently to strengthen our own thing. As a result, no change or innovation is sparked. We just sit at home in our pajama pants complaining about how wack everyone else is.

No idea is original. Reinventing the wheel is as futile as creating another music video show for BET. The Roots, as hip-hoppers should, were calling for freshness. When it comes to expressing ourselves, we might be surprised at what we find when we look inward.

I would have never looked good in those Skidz pants. They were unflattering on my young curves, and the colors looked hideous on my skin tone. A fool in cheap clothing.

6. Friends

ARTIST: WHODINI
ALBUM: ESCAPE (1984)

I KNOW A lot of people. No bull. I have tons of associates and professional contacts. If I go to a party, chances are there are people in the spot who I can wave to or give the "what's up" nod. Lots of folks call on me for favors, and I have a nice stable of dudes I used to date who I'm cordial with. But I can count on both hands, without exhausting all of my ten fingers, the number of true friends that I have.

This fact was made Vodka-clear during a recent birthday when I invited a dozen or so friends and associates to have drinks to celebrate. I wasn't expecting all of the busy New Yorkers to clear their hectic schedules for little ol' me, but I also wasn't expecting one friend to show up, leave early, and another to arrive at the sexy Uptown spot just before I decided to call the pitiful night quits. If I didn't feel insecure about my social popularity before that night, you best believe that pathetic feelings swept over me. How many friends do I really have?

Whodini's "Friends" captures this dilemma expertly. On top of a track that sounds like the best in '80s R&B, the oldie-but-goodie group explores what a true friend really is, while dismantling wannabe relationships:

the friends who catch the vapors, the backstabbing girlfriend who steals your man, and the sex-before-we-knew-each-other phenomenon. Alone, the song's hook airs my discontent by asking the question, "How many of us have them?"

Part of this frustration has to do with the fact that I can't tolerate a large magnitude of drama with the people I consider friends. Perhaps if I could accept the BS that arrogant diva Toni dished to her best friend Joan on the show *Girlfriends*, I wouldn't be writing this. Instead I choose to cut selfish folks off like the cable company.

That's not to say I'm not forgiving. I put my friends on mile-high pedestals. Unlike family members, where we have no choice in the selection process, we can handpick our friends and vice versa. While I'm not necessarily expecting them to jump in front of a bullet for me, I do expect a deep level of respect and understanding.

In a short clip from his documentary "Black and White: A Portrait of Sean Combs," Diddy said, "I don't have a lot of friends. I think people think I have a lot of friends. I don't think I really make a good friend." Despite the fact that millions want to get close to the hip-hop mogul, their reasons are more or less self-centered. As a result, Sean, who probably spends more time brokering deals than sharing intimate moments, finds it hard to relate to people below the surface. Thank God, I can't relate to that. But it's reassuring (and sad) to know that no matter on what rung of society's popularity ladder we stand, fostering significant relationships remains challenging.

For that reason, many of us cling to friendships with folks who we know bring us down. One of the standard excuses that we use is that we've known our homies since we were kids buying five-cent candy together. But what's time got to do with it? The real question is whether or not this person adds positive value to your life, a creditor not a debtor. Periodically, I evaluate the people in my personal cipher to ensure that those closest to me aren't smiling in my face while simultaneously plotting my downfall, like Bishop-versus-Q-style in the 1992 Tupac–Omar Epps film *Juice*.

My father once told me that if I had more than three friends, chances are I had too many. I don't necessarily agree that I have to cap my friends' lists, nor do I accept the cyberworld definition of a friend, where in one click of a button you've fostered a new relationship. I wonder how many of my hundreds of online "buddies" would have celebrated birthday drinks with me.

Even though I can comfortably fit my close friends in my family's Camry, I know that these people are willing to ride with me no matter what, no matter where. They believe in me. They trust me. They don't judge me. They love me. So when I hear Whodini ask the hard question, I need to answer proudly, "I do. It may be a small crew, but each member is priceless."

7. Brown Skin Lady

ARTIST: BLACK STAR

ALBUM: MOS DEF AND TALIB KWELI ARE BLACK STAR (1998)

I **DON'T HAVE** a weave. My hair has never run down my back. In fact, I don't have flippable hair. My mane is quite thick; without a perm it hurts when I comb through it. I might be able to pass the brown paper bag test because of my apple-juice complexion, but I'm clearly of color. I cannot pass. I don't want to.

When I skim through popular women's magazines or turn on the television, it's obvious that beauty standards were not established based on my blueprint. Sexy is the ability to flip one's hair. Sexy is light-skinned—or even better, white. Sexy is sickeningly thin. When many women look into the mirror, their reflection isn't one celebrated on billboards, in music videos, and on magazine covers. Many females go to great lengths to alter their design to fit a mold that was never really meant for them. Some women have been wearing weaves since their first period, like a rite of passage, while others starve themselves or hide their bodies under clothing barriers. Some just avoid mirrors and pray for nonexistence.

Sometimes when I walk the streets, turn on the radio, or overhear conversations, I forget that I'm picturesque even though I rock a short 'fro and my hips sway with the wind. Black Star's "Brown Skin Lady" is my reminder. A hip-hop tribute to women of color (no doubt a son of the influential Jungle Brothers's "Black Woman"), from the surface of their skin to the depth of their souls, Talib Kweli and Mos Def tell me that they like the way I walk. They like the way I move. They like the range of my sistas' colored complexions. Kweli reminds me that I'm "God's design." It means something coming from the rhymes of my brother.

On the song's track notes Talib Kweli wrote, "Too often, hip hop artists make songs about women with conditions. You know like, 'you my boo but you can't see no dough,' or 'if you get out of line, I have to smack you,' or they talk about how non-black looking the woman is. . . . We just wanted to do a song that celebrated women of color with no conditions, just because we love them." If only there were more love letters like "Brown Skin Lady" to counterbalance the negative and conformist images of females that bombard women on a daily basis.

Despite what glossy magazine covers depict, even if your hair has never flowed down your back and your skin is permanently kissed by the sun, there are plenty of people who admire your internal and external loveliness. But it's most important that you see it for yourself.

This brown-skin lady with knotty hair had to learn to embrace my own definition of beauty and firmly grip my self-worth. Regardless of what the media celebrates or how American culture wants to portray me, I'm in love with myself. My hair. My complexion. My mind. My design is exquisite. I like the way I move, too.

8. Afro Puffs

ARTIST: THE LADY OF RAGE, FEATURING SNOOP DOGGY DOGG
ALBUM: *ABOVE THE RIM: THE SOUNDTRACK* (1994)

WHAT MAKES A woman feminine? Is it the precise amount of perfume in the right places? Is it being waxed where hair shouldn't be? Is it perfectly manicured fingernails? Is it the presence of pink in one's wardrobe? Or is it the desire to shake one's apple bottom at the right tempo in the right direction?

If this is the case, I'm achieving a below-C average in the femininity department. I do shake it on occasion and I'm sure I get points for my shoe addiction. I'm not dainty. I don't like pink. I've been known to kick it with my boy, smoke a Black & Mild while blasting Beanie Sigel. I'm the quintessential homegirl (which isn't good for my chances of marriage, but that's a conversation for another day), and I've asked for barber recommendations on several occasions. I've even rocked my hair in a Caesar because it's a womanly joy to wake up, brush, and go.

But ain't I a woman?

I may shoot you a middle finger if I get one more comparison to Sanaa Lathan's FHF (female hip-hop fan) character in the movie *Brown Sugar.*

Apparently, the FHF who actually likes hip-hop (not just drops it to the current song that asks her to do so) is supposed to look (flannels and Tims?) and act a certain way (hardcore?). And I, like Lathan's character, don't fit the mold.

I hung out with a weed-smoking chef a few months back, and on the way to the lounge the local radio station was spinning a serious classic hip-hop mix. The kind of mix that you rarely hear these days. The type that you used to record with a cheap tape deck by holding down the record button. The chef was impressed that I could recite the lyrics to Black Moon's "How Many MC's. . . ." I was surprised that he was surprised. I thought he was going to give me a hand clap. He didn't. Don't most hip-hop fans know lines from the song? Isn't Black Moon's *Enta da Stage* a must-have album in the hip-hop fan's collection, right alongside Mobb Deep's *The Infamous*? Apparently so, but not for an FHF.

The first time I heard the Lady of Rage spit was on Dr. Dre's *The Chronic*, an album that's so testosterone-heavy it feels funny listening to it if you don't have anything to grab between your legs. You can actually smell the man-ness the moment the first beat drops. *Hint: it's the odor of a dude who just ran several games of street ball, then guzzled down a beer and smoked two blunts.* I liked the album nonetheless, even with the multi-platinum misogyny. When I heard Rage hold her own on the disturbing banger "Stranded on Death Row," I was like Squeak in *The Color Purple* asking Harpo, "Who dis woman?"

A thick sista with two large ponytails, Rage dropped "Afro Puffs" in

1994. She rhymes with dragon fire that she rocks "rough and stuff"" over a signature West Coast track that's bass-heavy, gangsta-infused, and equipped with hardcore bells and whistles. Even with Snoop Doggy Dogg's permission to "rock on," Rage's delivery and lyricism control the track. She has the audacity to flip the most bothersome aspects of womanhood and turn them into a virtue. Soaked in hip-hop's stickiest confidence, she raps that she flows like a menstrual cycle and labels any punk who tries to cramp her style as a "Pamprin child." It was obvious that she could go (un)manicured toe-to-toe with any (male) MC.

I felt everything about her. I liked the way she wore her femininity. There are times when I want to flaunt my own rage like a new purse.

Rage's delivery—a managed conflict between being a woman, being aggressive, and defining femininity on her own terms—is a nod to the female rap architects who hailed before her—Latifah, Lyte, Salt-N-Pepa. Nowadays, mainstream hip-hop's visual representations of femininity are severely limited to the sexual gratification of Lil' Kim and, uh, the sexual desires of a champagne-drenched groupie. Rage is a preexisting alternative that I can still get with. And I'm sure she had to deal with her share of sexism as an inmate on Death Row Records during Suge Knight's reign. Many women are stuck in all-boys clubs and struggle to maneuver while being comfortable in their own feminine skin.

I'm the only person I know who owns Rage's album *Necessary Roughness*, which was released three years after "Afro Puffs." To this day, I throw it on as feminine ginseng to give me energy to deal with the plight of womanhood coupled with ambition. Her music supports the notion that femininity is an abstract concept defined by the individual. The career, likes and dislikes, and appearance of a woman are not mutually exclusive. If folks can't accept my personal femininity, as Rage professed, "tough titty."

9. God Made Me Funke

ARTIST: KOOL MOE DEE
ALBUM: KOOL MOE DEE GREATEST HITS (1993)

BESIDES BEING CUTE, the Lawd has blessed me with a flair for words, a drive like Toyota, and a fine backside. So I say thank ya! I know, I know. Most of you are thinking, *She sure is blessed.* And I am! But, beloved, so are you! We all possess special gifts from the Creator. Sister Johnson is a beast in the kitchen, and Brother Ali plays the organ like nobody's business. And you know what else? God even made Kool Moe Dee funky. Y'all may not know about him, but I suggest you look him up. That's right. Mr. Dee, a rapper, has acknowledged his God-given talents. I think we all should, too.

Okay, maybe this isn't a real testimony that I would give on a Sunday morning at church, but the sentiment is genuine. "God Made Me Funke" is Kool Moe Dee's hip confession to The One Above for being "saved by the beat." Cool as he wanna be, the hip-hop originator gives praises to whom they were due.

My friends have mentioned on more than one occasion that they admire the way I put words together. After I blush, I remind them of their own unique talents, of which I'm equally fascinated. As a graphic designer, my boy José can whip up a visual representation of any concept. His artistic abilities are awesome. I can barely color in the lines, much less create fine art. My girl Sai, a corporate finance queen, is numerically and technically astute; an incredible problem solver as well as a wiz at finding the best travel deals around (everyone should have a friend who can find the cheapest way to get the hell out of Dodge). As a doctor, my girl Dominique has the ability to heal people. *Heal people?* Heavy.

There's always a tendency to covet gifts that we don't have. When I'm in the shower auditioning for *American Idol*, practicing my performance piece, "Sweet Thing," which Chaka Khan killed vocally, I resent the fact that I can't sing like Jill Scott, Patti LaBelle, Anita Baker, or Ashanti, for that matter. After hearing me blow, my mother gently said, "We all need hobbies." God made me funky in the way that I was to be funkdafied.

Everyone is blessed with a special talent. Their thing. Their gift. This genius may not always be apparent, because sometimes we can't remain quiet enough to stumble upon it or passionate enough to pursue it. Sometimes these talents require us to tap into them without fear, which in itself is scary. But there's nothing more tragic than wasted blessings. It's like sitting on top of a pile of money and doing just that, chilling.

Each morning, I have to say thank ya for my blessings. I embrace the gifts that I've received and use them to the fullest. I write and I pray and I pray and I write. I am thankful that I can eat off my words. God didn't just make Kool Moe Dee "funke." We all got a little somethin', somethin' worth sharing with the world.

10. *Young, Gifted and Black*

ARTIST: BIG DADDY KANE
ALBUM: IT'S A BIG DADDY THING (1989)

IF I WERE given a chance to speak in front of the entire hip-hop generation, I would spend my four minutes discussing self-esteem. Some of you may be thinking, *Self-esteem? What about violence, misogyny, political mobilization? One of our problems is that these rappers are too cocky.*

Think about it. If I dedicated my soapbox speech to self-esteem and self-love, I would also be addressing violence, misogyny, and other ills that plague hip-hoppers. Many of our problems can be traced back to how we view and think about ourselves. And, subsequently, how we let the views of others dictate our lives.

Need more evidence? Turn on a rap video and you'll get a front-row show where our pathologies drop it like it's hot. Young women with cheeks hanging out are proud to be visibly invisible as they grind to the bassline. Meanwhile, young men pay homage to the block, reenact shootouts, and star in their own crack fables. When's the last time you saw a hip-hop video that took place at a school graduation? Or that celebrated hip-hoppers for being young and gifted? Our devastating self-images are as rooted as the fields that slaves used to plow for their lives.

When the music videos go off and we stop dancing, we find ourselves in dysfunctional relationships and demeaning jobs. We sit in the backseat while someone else navigates our potential toward a dead end.

Nearly twenty years ago, Big Daddy Kane took a page from Nina Simone's songbook and combined three powerful weapons: young, gifted, and black. To reflect Kane's spiritual connections, "Young, Gifted and Black" begins with a snippet from a Minister Farrakhan speech where he speaks of calling an "individual into existence." Many of us don't believe we have a divine calling on our lives, so we squander them. Some of us are told that we're not exceptional, so we act accordingly. "Young, Gifted and Black" is Kane's calm scream to the world, and to other MCs, of course, that he's a walking contribution with immense talent. He's young. He's gifted. He's black. He knows it. He feels it.

People with healthy self-images are forces to be reckoned with. Not only do they love themselves, they respect the person that they are, which means they require the same regard from others. People with high self-esteem know that they have a divine mission and exude a strong sense of pride, regardless of their sex, ethnicity, or other "determinant." And dare I say it, they are *happy*. Imagine if every member of the hip-hop community felt this way. BET would look very different.

After my soapbox speech, I would ask the hip-hop community to gather in a circle as we hold hands and repeat, *I am somebody*. Naw, just playing. Instead the DJ would spin "Young, Gifted and Black" precisely at the moment when Kane spits, "The message I got to give is a benefit for you and me."

11. *Peer Pressure*

ARTIST: MOBB DEEP
ALBUM: JUVENILE HELL (1993)

PEER PRESSURE IS usually equated with our younger days when the cool kid offered us some drugs (unless you were said cool kid), the fine basketball player wanted to "get closer," or the homeboys urged us to "become a man."

When "Peer Pressure" was released in the early '90s, Queensbridge representers Mobb Deep were dwelling in the juvenile hell of their inner-city environment, a microcosm of the bigger hell known as adulthood. In young Prodigy's world, stress is constant. His parents tell him to finish school. He doesn't know how to follow their advice and still be embraced by his beer-sipping, fly-gear-wearing partners. If Prodigy wants to be down, he'll have to find a way to make lots of cash fast. He wants to be an architect, but that dream will have to be put on hold. Sound familiar? Young Havoc relates an all too common tale about a guy around the way who hides his intellect because we all know that smart guys finish last, right? The smart dumb kid goes from an "A" average to acting like a "savage" on the streets. Living destructively becomes too heavy; with a burner and a note, the smart troubled kid ends the pressure forever.

Fast-forward to adulthood and I see the same pressure, which has only aged, affecting grown folks. Our desire to amass whips and chains in order to look impressive on *MTV Cribs*. Our need to submerge parts of ourselves in order to fit in at work. Ask a grown Havoc and Prodigy about the peer pressure in the music industry to project a certain type of image. Through this aged pressure, the end goal remains the same: an older version of the juvenile desire to be accepted and hang out with the cool people on the block.

As youngsters it can be hard to hold on to convictions and beliefs; the necessary maturity may not have developed. It should be expected, though, that as adults we would be able to devise grown ways to avoid succumbing to pressure. But what I've found is that adulthood illuminates the understanding that "just say no" is really just a simple solution to a complex problem.

It works for me to act from the heart. I usually never go wrong. I may not always make the popular choice, but I make one that I can live with. Mobb Deep sum up our reality: "You gotta find a way to deal" with the pressure so that we don't abandon our dreams, make destructive decisions, or lose hope. Wise words from the mouths of youngstas.

12. You Know My Steez

ARTIST: GANG STARR
ALBUM: MOMENT OF TRUTH (1998)

I'VE BEEN TOLD that I've got a mean strut. I know it. And I usually whip it out at opportune times, like on the way to a money meeting, arm-in-arm with a date, or whenever I wear heels. My walk is a mix of confidence, a dash of arrogance, and lots of pride. Each step screams, "I'm unstoppable." I look folks in the eye along the way, as if to say, "What?"

In hip-hop some would call this swagger. According to Urban Dictionary (www.urbandictionary.com), a Web site that's compiled by anyone who has an Internet connection, swagger is defined as "how one presents him or herself to the world"; "prideful, arrogant walk or stride"; "person's style—the way they walk, talk, dress"; and "conceited attitude, cockiness, arrogance." You know swagger when you see it walk down the street, enter a room, or command an audience.

Swagger is usually reserved for men. It's Billy Dee Williams in *Lady Sings the Blues*. It's Terrence Howard in everything. It's Dwyane Wade's drive to the dunk. It's the unconventional attraction to Jay-Z. Unfortunately, a select group of rappers have twisted swagger into an unofficial and uninspired (yawn) sport of who's got the biggest penis.

And some female rappers have unsuccessfully translated it into the baddest broad syndrome.

"You Know My Steez" is a tribute to Gang Starr's swagger, to the unique style that they embody with ease. Their steez is a mix of intellectually gritty rhymes and hard-hitting tracks. And as Guru says before the song drops, part of Gang Starr's style is that their art is laced with a message. Their swagger on wax is mentally attractive.

My swagger also delves beyond the visual and the physical. I embrace it to help me navigate the world. As warrior writer Jill Nelson once affirmed, "It's hard out here for a sister." So my internal confidence is one of my most powerful weapons I have to smash ceilings, slice stereotypes, and silence fear. My swagger in action is like a b-girl freeze: proud, confident, ill. I flaunt it. In meetings. In front of audiences. My steez is the representation of knowing that I'm powerful: mind, body, and spirit.

True swagger isn't a hard bop or an isolated act of confidence. It's being self-assured in who you are and what you have to offer beyond your magic stick or your candy shop. Swagger is about letting that inner confidence shine whether you have a dollar in your pocket or millions in the bank. Swagger is provoking others to believe in you.

Gang Starr had more than ten years in the game. Accident? Nope. We know their steez. Does the world know yours?

13. Rebirth of Slick *(Cool Like Dat)*

ARTIST: DIGABLE PLANETS
ALBUM: REACHIN' (A NEW REFUTATION OF TIME AND SPACE) (1993)

IN MIDDLE AND high school, and even in college, for that matter, I can't say I was cool. I wasn't corny. I don't think. I dressed aight, rocked my share of short skirts and high-heeled boots. I had a fairly healthy social life and a fine boyfriend who chicks started to sweat after I got with him. However, I think if my schoolmates were to think of cool, my picture would not pop up in their mind. I was too nerdy between my advanced placement classes in high school and the high grade point average I carried in college. And I didn't bother sweating the popular folks. I was not cool in the way that it was defined at that time.

"Rebirth of Slick" was like nothing I had heard or seen before. Yeah, we had some jazzy rap previously, but Digable Planets's execution seemed much more deliberate. The song is unusually abstract and didn't make much sense to me growing up. I didn't catch all their references (had no clue who Cleopatra Jones was at the time), but the beat was head-nodding. The two males of the group, Butterfly and Doodlebug, were cuties. Ladybug was a dope (female) MC. I liked their style (had no idea they were sampling the Last Poets). Although their rhymes flew above my head, they had me reachin'. Truly grown and sexy.

When "Rebirth of Slick" was released in 1993, hip-hop was in the middle of a gangster's paradise. Cool, at this hip-hop point, was increasingly violent, stereotypical, and limiting. So three open-minded MCs who referred to themselves as bugs and planets crafted their own definition and implied that anyone could do the same.

As I approach the end of my twenties, I'm experiencing my own rebirth of slick. My personal cool is emerging, and it is, for lack of a better term, grown and sexy. Not the "no tennis shoes at the club" type, but an assertive, sharp, and independent embodiment. I no longer strive to be cool for cool's sake. Cool isn't afraid of books or the History Channel. Cool is a ten-dollar dress from a secondhand store. Cool is intelligent, funky, and individualistic like Digable Planets's style of hip-hop and reflects their moniker, which was derived from the members' belief that each person is his or her own planet. Welcome to mine.

Cool may be entirely different to you. It may be cowboy boots, the cooking channel, and chess. It may be manga, marathons, and miniskirts. It's up to you to define. That's cool.

14. *Liberation*

ARTIST: OUTKAST, FEATURING CEE-LO, ERYKAH BADU, AND BIG RUBE
ALBUM: AQUEMINI (1998)

IMAGINE A LIFE where you're free to be your complete self. All the complex, contradictory, and beautiful pieces of you. Imagine a life where nothing or no one, including yourself, holds you back from pursuing your dreams. Imagine a life where you choose your destiny regardless of your location on the socioeconomic ladder or the racial map. Imagine a life where the only thoughts that truly matter are yours.

One of the most profound OutKast songs is an opus, a musical masterpiece in which the Hotlanta duo invites their talented friends to explore the various degrees of freedom. "Liberation" is the song to throw on when you're tired, confused, agitated, hungry, on the brink, challenged, suffering, happy, sad, defeated, or victorious. With a melodic piano framework that's draped with percussions, Andre muses that he wants the kind of liberation where he doesn't care what others think. Big Boi reveals the power that his family instilled in him to be whoever he wanted to be. The unboxable Cee-Lo takes you to church, where his soul sings, "We alive, but we ain't living." The funky Erykah Badu assesses the psychotic price of fame and its opposition to liberating minds. And poet

Big Rube concludes with a spoken word joint that encapsulates a multi-dimensional struggle.

In the middle of OutKast's colossal composition is an emotional call to action to release the shackles that bind us and to "shake that load off."

Then the beat rides to give you time to contemplate your own path to liberation. And that's when I realize (again) that as much as I like to think that I'm free, there are many factors—from self-doubt to genetic makeup—that stand in my way. With the beat still in the background, I conclude (again) that none of these reasons should prevent me from living without limits.

The life that we imagined above is available for the taking, if we believe. Are our minds free enough to accept the possibility?

What better group than OutKast to explore the complexity of freedom? Big Boi and Andre champion doing their own thing. When they first appeared on the scene, they were a southern group eager for respect in an East and West Coast hip-hop game, but still brought the heat even if other regions were too shallow to notice. As time passed, within their group dynamic they've allowed themselves to pursue personal artistic ambitions, which was evident in the release of their double-disc CD *Speakerboxxx/The Love Below*. Andre's on a fiery mission to express his individualism, reinventing himself as often as Madonna. He went from jeans and jerseys to blond wigs and furry pants. None of which has undermined his brilliance as an artist. Can he live?

Individuality scares us. But in pursuing our own liberation, we have to step aside and let others do the same. It's harder to open our minds than it is our mouths. I don't know too many people who have reached the level of freedom where they don't worry about what others think. I don't know too many people who don't fear branching out into a new direction and are unafraid of how people will react. I know only a handful of folks who give up the safe route to pursue the dirt road that takes considerably longer than the paved one.

My aim is a free existence. And with each spin of "Liberation" I realize I'm getting closer. I want the life imagined above. I may have to become an outcast to do it, but freedom is worth it.

15. *Can't Stop This*

ARTIST: THE ROOTS
ALBUM: GAME THEORY (2006)

IN **JEFF CHANG'S** *Can't Stop Won't Stop: A History of the Hip-Hop Generation*, he writes that Grandmaster Flash refused to meet with record executives who wanted to sign him and his crew, the Furious Five, because the pioneer didn't think anyone would purchase a rap record.

Fast-forward more than thirty years after hip-hop's organic inception and we're everywhere: in boardrooms, on television, and in classrooms. Some of us may be clothed in suits, fireman uniforms, or boho gear, but we're still representing, despite all the rah-rah that said we'd never make it. We're still here.

As hip-hoppers we've suffered our share of growing pains and black eyes. Many didn't think we'd make it this far without a defined political movement fighting for us, just as many doubted the longevity of a culture that rose from the concrete. No one thought hip-hop would be studied by academics, just as folks dismissed our desires to break into new career fields like fashion, movies, and literature. People are surprised that we're running companies. And some still don't want to acknowledge that many of us are mobilizing grassroots organizations to effect change in our communities. Early on, journalists, record executives, and businesspeople looked at hip-hoppers like we were faceless. Now we're seen. They changed their tune to hip-hop; our global influence is undeniable. From the South Bronx to South America.

"Can't Stop This" is eight minutes of celebrating hip-hop—the good, the bad, and the real. It's also a tribute to the late, supertalented musician J Dilla and the positive influence he's had on a crop of hip-hoppers, not just from a musical standpoint. His legacy lives on through hip-hop. Forever.

Despite the personal obstacles that we've all faced in this journey called life—including the death of loved ones, the tribulations of making it, and the struggle to emerge—we keep going like the hands of a clock. We're living. Breathing. Trying. Achieving. Rhyming. Growing. Dreaming. We ain't going nowhere.

We continue to face challenges with more dark hours to come. But right now we should take time to delight in the shortsightedness of those who didn't think we would be here today. In fact, throw on your favorite hip-hop song or pump "Can't Stop This," groove to your longevity, and celebrate your successes. Dance to your individual potential and celebrate hip-hop's collective one. Revel in the fact that you don't stop. We don't stop.

Cashmere
Thoughts

PART TWO

16. *Back in the Day* (Remix)

ARTIST: AHMAD
ALBUM: AHMAD (1994)

WHEN **I WAS** a youngster, my life revolved around whether or not I would be able to go outside and play with my friends. Talk about stressful. I had to wait for my mother to come home from work, which, if I was lucky, was around 5:30 p.m., and, if I wasn't, wouldn't be until late in the evening. With each passing moment, I hoped my friends weren't having fun without me. I cursed life for being unfair.

The one and only song that I can name by Ahmad (who has since gone on to become a member of the "hiprocksoul" group 4th Avenue Jones) is an ode to the good old days when life was easy. Using a sample from Teddy Pendergrass's "Love T.K.O.," Ahmad wraps you in nostalgia and brings you back to those warm times when you would get mad at your best friend for five minutes but quickly move on without a hint of bad feelings. A golden era. The nasal-voiced rapper reminisces about his childhood, when in 1985 he was around ten years old, riding bikes, playing the dozens, and imagining the day when he'd be grown. But now, as an adult, he wishes that all he had to do was finish his homework. He wishes he could be young again. I feel the kid.

When we were ten we wanted to be sixteen. When we were sixteen we wanted to be eighteen. When we were eighteen we wanted to be twenty-one. And it's at that point we want to freeze time. When did things become complicated? Now that I'm here, in adulthood, I should have heeded Momma's advice when she said I should cherish my younger years. I never understood what "growing pains" meant until I started to feel those sharp jabs in my sides as I dealt with a career, relationships, and responsibilities. I can no longer blame mistakes on the naiveté of youth.

The instant I found out that life only gets harder it seemed like it all went downhill. That is, until I realized that I was wasting precious moments yearning for times long past while the present drifted by. I had to learn how to appreciate my adulthood. And start loving it.

Many of us long for those older days instead of embracing the present. We're broke down in the past and have no desire to move on. We lie about our age, dread upcoming birthdays, and put immense pressure on ourselves because we don't have 2.5 kids, the picket fence, and the marriage by the time we reach thirty. It doesn't help that hip-hop feasts on nostalgia and embraces young attitudes. Growing up is no longer cool.

Just because we have to grow up—and, yes, we all have to at some point in our lives—doesn't mean we can't enjoy some of the aspects of being young. Adulthood can make us so serious. There are times when we should put the responsibilities to the side and let our only concern be how soon we can make it outside to play and enjoy being grown.

17. *Wear Clean Draws*

ARTIST: THE COUP
ALBUM: PARTY MUSIC (2001)

MY MOTHER DID a wonderful job of shielding me from the world's ugliness. She did tell me that there would be bad days. She did tell me that there are people who will want to hurt me. Reluctantly, she let me go into the world equipped with a good head on my shoulders and stellar home training.

Once I reached the real world, I wish Momma would have told me about the racists who smile in your face, the individuals who go to great lengths to kill your spirit, and the people who harbor hate like a fugitive. Much of which I had to learn the hard way. I don't know about you, but I don't necessarily need to experience something to learn from it.

There's a tendency for parents to sugarcoat the world as an easy-to-swallow placebo. It makes perfect sense. Why scare your children? The hope is that your babies won't have to face any of these monsters, so why talk about them and call them into existence?

The basis of the Coup's "Wear Clean Draws" is a piece of advice that many parents bestow upon their children. My mother told me, and her mother probably told her: *Wear clean panties every day. God forbid you're hit by a car and you're sent to the hospital. You don't want to be embarrassed by having on unsightly draws.* When you think about it, it's a comical adage. If you're like me and you wind up in the emergency room, you'd probably be more concerned with how the hell you're going to pay for your visit (does health insurance cover it?). Not with whether you have on the underwear with the hole in the front.

This is the disconnect that we sometimes experience when we leave the safety of our parents' house and enter the "real world." Clean draws is one thing. Securing health insurance is another.

The Coup's front man, Boots Riley, rhymes to his daughter typical advice that parents pass down to their children, like "Brush your teeth after every meal" and "Wash your hands after you go to the bathroom." But he also remixes the wisdom with a revolutionary tone to give her an early introduction to what she's up against. He tells her to beware of the bosses that take money from the people, and if she plays house she should "pretend that the man clean up." It's both handy and modernized advice given over a funky track that feels like a breezy summer day in Brooklyn's Prospect Park.

As Boots says, "the world ain't no fairy tale." The streets can be mean. Ivy League schools can be mean. Corporate America can be mean. We've got to be both practical and radical, building upon the advice of our parents, shedding those words of wisdom that no longer apply—like, "Stand by your wo(man) no matter what," and the "doctor-lawyer-engineer" rule of thumb—and adding the wisdom we gain from our real-world experiences. We need a strong foundation but we also have to be sharp,

inquisitive, and challenging to deal with characters like Big Bad Pharma or Da Tax Man.

I throw my underwear away when they have holes in them, become worn out, or would under any circumstance embarrass me if a hospital employee were to see them. I will tell my children to do the same. And I'll also tell my kids that whether they like it or not, they're going to need some health insurance.

18. The Choice Is Yours (Revisited)

ARTIST: BLACK SHEEP
ALBUM: A WOLF IN SHEEP'S CLOTHING (1991)

AS A KID, I used to love that game show *Let's Make a Deal*. While the contestants' silly costumes and the host's corny jokes amused my young self, what I liked most about the show was the high-pressured decision making. I would play along, shouting, "Pick door number two!" If you were good at making choices, you were a winner. Isn't that an underlying rule in life?

"The Choice Is Yours," which landed Black Sheep on the hip-hop map, is an indisputable classic that if the DJ at a club spins it at the precise moment, the entire party will jump up and down. Dres and Mista Lawnge offer two options: this or that. "This" is Black Sheep's witty brand of hip-hop. "That" is everything else. Not on a better-than-thou tip, but through clever rhyming, Dres reveals that he's made the decision to do music the way he feels inside. He's going to swing it his way, and it doesn't matter if you like it, because he's got his own back. It's his prerogative.

The video takes the concept a step further. "That" becomes social and political ills as images of drugs, violence, and the KKK flash across the screen to represent the myriad of destructive options available to us. A conscious decision on their part, Black Sheep's use of political messages shows that even a party song can serve a larger purpose.

Life can be broken down into a series of choices. Once I tried to count the number of times I had to make a decision throughout the day—from waking up and deciding what to eat for breakfast, to selecting what trains to take to an appointment, to choosing what greens (collards, kale, string beans?) I should heat from a can to accompany my fried chicken. After a while keeping track became too overwhelming; I lost count and gave up.

On one hand, it's jive liberating that our lives are molded by our decisions. The choice really is ours. We can define our path. We can decide the type of life we want to lead. We can choose our profession, our friends, our mates. We can choose to return to school. We can choose to pursue our true passion. Of course there are other factors like environmental and social ones to consider, but at the rawest level it is *choice* that gives us power. We do have control in this volatile world.

It's also a helluva lot of pressure. Choice becomes scary. If we are in control, then bad decisions we make that land us in dark-alley situations are our fault. We are responsible for our plight. We can fly or we can sink. The sooner we accept the fact that we may not always pick the right road, the sooner we can release some of the pressure of selecting. It is our prerogative.

When offered three doors, we may not always select the one beaming with opportunity. Instead we may opt for the one with a wheelbarrow full of fried manure. That's when we have to ask ourselves, *Did I at least learn something to prevent me from choosing that dead-end door again? Can I at least walk away from this situation better than when I first stepped into it?*

People laugh at me, but there are times when faced with a dilemma that I break out an old-school pros and cons list to weigh my options. I've made some bad decisions. I mean ones where even I don't know what the hell I was thinking. But I can proudly say that my mistakes weren't in vain. A sista is learning. I'm exerting my prerogative with intellect and heart and gaining confidence in my ability to select the right door.

19. *Stressed Out*

ARTIST: A TRIBE CALLED QUEST, FEATURING CONSEQUENCE AND FAITH EVANS
ALBUM: BEATS, RHYMES AND LIFE (1996)

LAST MONTH **I** almost lost my mind. While checking myself out in the mirror, making sure everything was in order, I noticed a silver speck sticking out of the side of my head. Upon closer inspection it looked like a gray hair. Before freaking out, I pulled on the silver suspect to make sure it wasn't just a piece of lint from my pillow.

It wasn't a piece of lint. It was a strand of gray hair. And I'm not even thirty.

I proceeded to freak out and then engaged in a sixty-second recap on the current stressors in my life. I wanted culprits. I wanted to blame something (or somebody). What I came up with—work, pending move, and recent relationship issues—didn't add up to enough, in my mind, to nurture a gray hair. Those demands are pretty habitual, normal. I started to really freak out.

Truth is, I really don't have any one proven, effective method to deal with stress. Yeah, I've tried fake meditative breathing that I saw on television. But I'm not one of those centered chicks who can brush off the obstacles of life with one tight yoga move. I tend to linger over my problems like I'm getting paid for it.

I find solace in knowing that I'm not the only one. "Stressed Out" is one of the shining tracks of A Tribe Called Quest's *Beats, Rhymes and Life* album. Q-Tip (too bad Phife's not on the track) and comeback-in-the-making rapper Consequence discuss the daily struggles of making it and how adversities threaten to knock us down. The severely underrated Faith Evans enters the track with her soothing voice to tell us that she knows how we feel.

I've never met anyone who's never experienced stress. That would be one superpower I wouldn't mind possessing. We all seem to have our own way of (not) dealing with it. I know people who pray. I know people who lean on friends. I know people who make jokes. I have friends who cry. I have friends who exercise.

I also know people who drink. I know people who overeat. I know people who shop. I know people who smoke cigarettes. I've done all of the above and then some.

These days I converse with my stress and treat it like an unwanted lover. "Why are you here," I'll ask. "Don't you have someone else you could be bothering?" After a little back and forth, I try to be firm and say, "You don't have to go home, but you have to get the hell out of here."

What's funny is that before I kick my stress out (believe me, most of the time it is a struggle; sometimes I want to get the police involved), it tells me that I am the one who invited it in the first place.

Guilty as charged. I usher stress into my life and give it a seat in my mind like I work at a Broadway theater. Just as Consequence rapped, I'm caught up over securing the American dream, only to realize late in the game that I don't even like picket fences. And now that I know that, I never feel like I'm moving fast enough to achieve my dream deferred. Allowing stress to occupy my space isn't going to push me to the place I want to be any quicker. It will only slow me down.

Freaking out over my strand of gray hair is doubly offensive and not to mention, stupid. Q-Tip rhymes simply, "Let that nonsense ride." And sometimes that's the most effective plan of attack.

20. Smile

ARTIST: SCARFACE, FEATURING 2PAC
ALBUM: THE UNTOUCHABLE (1997)

"**S**MILE," THE MIDDLE-AGED Latino man sweeping the floor said as he looked into my eyes. More often than not, I walk around with a mug on my face. I'm not necessarily angry. Smiling just isn't my default facial expression. But when the bodega employee added, "Don't ever let anyone steal your joy," I internalized what he said and fixed my face. Did I always look melancholy when I stopped in to pick up juice?

Many men have told me to smile as I walk the streets. Usually it's their wack attempt at flirting, so to keep the exchange short, I flash a grin, revert back to a frown, and keep it moving. But in the bodega that day, I realized that I needed to update how I present my face.

Too often we let our negative emotions consume us and take over our facial expressions. I'm not a naturally morose or angry person. I love to laugh, but for some reason I usually reserve laughter for the happy times, not for the rough ones. I can be caught rolling my eyes when some eternal optimist tells me to smile through the perfect storm. Easier said than done.

Women's magazines, in particular, have been infamous for regurgitating articles that mention laughter as a good way to fight the stressors of life. But this sentiment was made more powerful coming from 2Pac, probably because I know that his silver lining was tarnished throughout his short life. On the introduction to "Smile," which also features H-Town representer Scarface, 2Pac says that in life you have to retain a sense of humor despite the harsh obstacles that will come your way. He had a beautiful smile. I wonder how often he took his own advice.

Scarface's rhymes imply that many of us sport the perpetual frown because we still carry unresolved pain from our childhood.

Isn't the miracle behind the act of smiling enough—an awesome marvel in life's bigger picture? Perhaps that's a little corny. But we shouldn't give smiling a bad rap (excuse the pun). Some of us act like if we're caught performing this joyful act, we might catch a criminal charge. We shouldn't be afraid to sport happiness.

We may need to search for motivation to smile more often, and embrace it as a gift of living. For me, I've been told that I'm prettier when I smile. That's more than enough reason for me to sport a cheesy, class-picture grin everywhere I go.

21. Look Thru My Eyes

ARTIST: DMX
ALBUM: IT'S DARK AND HELL IS HOT (1998)

I ONCE HAD a girlfriend whose sexual reputation preceded her. To guys we knew, she was a ho, freak, slut, and even less popular insults. From the first day I met her it was obvious that the two of us were different. Yet we still clicked. She was outgoing, forward, and weird. She was also unafraid to disclose to a girl she had just met the number of sexual partners she had. The number was in the thirties. We were seventeen.

We hung. We partied. I got to know her. She was more than what the guys said. For her, sex was liberation. She thought she was exerting her prerogative. She thought she was in control. I knew she was full of it. She'd later tell me, nonchalantly, about her first sexual experience, which happened when she was thirteen. It wasn't consensual. He was older. It was at that moment that I actually understood her.

I don't have to read a profile in *XXL* to tell that DMX has been through some stuff. His hardened face and darkened eyes speak volumes. Hip-hop has given DMX a voice, and he uses it to paint his reality in all of its troubled truth and ugliness.

"Look Thru My Eyes" takes the walk-in-my-shoes argument to another level. DMX already knows we will hurt our feet if we trade places with him, but it's the only way we'll be able to understand why he does "dirt in the street." Without some level of compassion, it's hard to listen to a DMX album and understand the artistry, attitude, and arrogance behind songs about robbing that are alongside tracks dedicated to praying. Some have called this type of behavior (which we've seen in rappers as well as politicians) schizophrenic, and that may be valid, but I also see *It's Dark and Hell Is Hot* as DMX's troubled truth.

We all have flawed truths of varying degrees. Oftentimes these realities are so painful that we hardly uncover them or allow others to see through our eyes and into our souls. Instead, we mask our realities with self-destructive behavior like crime and promiscuity. People's actions are hardly ever rootless.

DMX wants us to experience what he's faced before we judge him. But that's not how it works, is it? Don't we perform twisted calculations where the lower the pants, the more likely he's involved in some criminal activity, and the higher the skirt, the more likely she's involved in some promiscuous activity?

I've done my share of surface reading. Gotten caught up in media and stereotypical hype. But how much does this behavior backfire on me? What do people think when they see a young black woman? I want people to look into my eyes, not at my clothes, my hair, or my skin. I want to be understood, not dismissed.

Long fingers have been pointed without the actual work it takes to understand the why behind a DMX. Understanding doesn't mean you necessarily are in agreement with or advocate someone's behavior. We don't have to defend DMX, but how can we expect people to gain consciousness, change their ways, and grow if all we do is condemn them? No, this isn't a defense of DMX. This is a defense of dialogue, understanding, compassion, and action. My friend didn't deserve to be called names—she deserved to be understood and helped.

22. *Hypocrite*

ARTIST: AKROBATIK
ALBUM: BALANCE (2003)

I'M A HYPOCRITE, and I'll bet two months' rent that you are, too. Rap music screams hypocrisies. It "touts" being real but projects false images. It reps the streets but forgets about those still struggling in the hood. It's recorded by some rappers who love their momma but clearly have a disdain for women.

Between the hooks of some hip-hop songs you can hear many of my own contractions. On a rainy day I may swear off the music when I hear an illiterate rapper call me a b$tch, and on a hot day I may dance to the same song if the volume's loud enough in the club. I hate how materialistic the hip-hop generation can be, but damn, I yearn for the day to be able to cop those six-hundred-dollar Gucci boots. Hypocrite? Yep.

Real recognizes real, and as Akrobatik told me, "I don't know anyone who's never been a hypocrite." After I performed a mental scan (my high school principal? Pops? me?), I had to agree. Sidebar: I don't know what to say to trigger-happy police officers, child-molesting priests, or crack-smoking politicians. They need to consult a higher power.

As I swim in fairly normal waters of contradictions, "Hypocrite" is as refreshing as a Snapple from the corner store. After the beat knocks, Boston-based lyricist Akrobatik enters with a forceful delivery. He doesn't serve the usual unproductive pointing-fingers stance. His perspective is inward and outward. Akrobatik runs down a list of everything he doesn't do: watch videos, drink liquor, talk smack, look down on his fellow man, or smoke cigarettes. But then he flips it, as acrobats do, and reveals that if you catch him doing any of the above, it's because he's a hypocrite and human.

Let's be clear. Neither Akrobatik nor I, for that matter, are advocating embracing hypocrisy and using it as a pardon. The song is his way of exposing the fact that although he makes conscious material, he isn't a holier-than-thou dude—he is, in essence, like you and me. "Hypocrite" is a lyrical blanket statement that he's just as likely to make a mistake or do something he may have never thought he would do. It is important for us to face our contradictions, the role they play in the making of who we are, and embark on a path to get them in alignment like planets.

It ain't easy. To congregate all of our beliefs in one nice agreement is like bonding your hip-hop family from over west with your feminist family over east. Everyone may not get along. To take it a step further and ensure that our actions mirror the thoughts that are safely floating in our minds produces another complex problem.

However, contradictions can be used as stakes to keep us grounded. They can help to limit our own judgments against other people. Akrobatik told me that he was tired of people's tendency to judge others before checking themselves. If you ain't perfect or Jesus, why try to project such a feat on someone else?

Whether I like it or not, my contradictions make me who I am. And all of them don't require a hush-your-mouth reaction. Some are as simple as being an independent woman and wanting a man to take care of me. But I have to be honest with myself. It's when we front and mask these internal conflicts that no progression or growth is achieved.

The important questions are: *How do we manage these contradictions? How honest are we with ourselves about our contradictions? How honest are we with the world about our conflicting and often changing ideals?*

It starts with acknowledgment and ownership and then segues into reconciliation. We may have to prioritize which of our actions and beliefs are most important and allow them to pull rank over others. The goal should always be to remain true to self, and surely everything else will fall into place.

23. *It's Like That*

ARTIST: RUN-D.M.C.
ALBUM: RUN-D.M.C. (1984)

ONE OF MY favorite lines to explain something and nothing at the same time is, "It is what it is." I've adopted the statement into my rhetoric repertoire to explain the most obscure and significant facts of life.

"It is what it is" represents a variation of Run-D.M.C.'s "It's Like That." In the song, the kings of rock don't pretend to know the reasons behind the dilemmas of the world, but they acknowledge that these circumstances reflect our reality. Money is necessary. People eventually die. We make less than what we owe. "It's like that" is followed by "and that's the way it is."

There are many realities that we can't change, most notably race and nationality. We can't change where we're from or who our family is. Some things are fixed, and spending precious time debating the unchangeable is rarely productive.

I remember sitting on a publishing panel where a volleyed discussion took place about the fact that black writers have it harder than their white counterparts. It doesn't take a genius to present that argument. I had to chime in. Isn't it usually the case that people of color have a harder time in several aspects of American society? Shouldn't we spend time discussing how we can affect the consequences of those circumstances? I wished Run-D.M.C. would have rolled up, jumped on stage, and shouted their simple credo to the audience.

There's a tendency to stop the discussion at uncovering the reality instead of taking the necessary steps toward challenge and change. We get caught in the web of rhetoric, very similar to the "it is harder for a black writer" discussion, which had more roundabouts than Washington, DC, but didn't involve any action plans. Recognition is important, yes, but it is only a primer for change.

I will be a black female writer until the day I die. I know this fact will continue to present challenges, but if I wallow in the pond of my reality, I'll never swim toward the oceans where I can effect change. I should head toward the body of opportunity where I can insert one more black female perspective into mainstream media while simultaneously encouraging others to do the same.

My sister's reality is that she's a single mother. I probably spend more time than she does upset at the circumstances. She doesn't have time to indulge woulda, coulda, or shoulda. She's too focused on raising her daughter to be a star. I can't sit around bothered by the inevitable: my niece has to grow up in this crazy world whether I like it or not. It's my job to make it easier for her.

24. I'm Bad

ARTIST: LL COOL J
FROM: BIGGER AND DEFFER (1987)

I USED TO be a member of the sickest dance group to ever do it. You've probably never heard of us. We went by the name P.S., which stood for Pookie (me) and Sai (my best friend, from three houses down). No one could tell us we weren't the hottest dance group out of West Orange, New Jersey, which in the '80s was not a breeding ground for hip-hop. Rocking matching jumpers, with one shoulder strap down, we knew we'd make it big one day and tour the country as backup dancers for various groups, including our favorite, Bell Biv DeVoe. Although our dance career ultimately ended in the seventh grade, we possessed unshakeable confidence. If we didn't think we were the hotness, why would anyone else?

LL Cool J thought he was sickwidit before he was legal, too. He burst onto the fledgling hip-hop scene as a teenager with an old arrogance. To this day, between the pounding beat and Todd's delivery, "I'm Bad" still rocks my bells. The Queens-bred rapper compares himself to everyone from Mike Tyson to Jaws. By the end of the song, you *believe* that he's one bad mofo.

Years later, becoming a fixture in one of the most fickle industries, LL dubbed himself the Muhammad Ali of rap and named one of his albums *G.O.A.T.* (Greatest of All Time). Debates about who's the best MC of all time will circulate for the life of hip-hop. Whether or not you agree with LL's claim, it's dumb obvious that his self-confidence had a lot to do with his ability to sustain a rap career that spans more than two decades. No one can ever take that from him.

This boastful attitude is innate to hip-hop culture. Run-D.M.C. donned themselves kings of rock and urged wack rappers to call them "sire." You can't tell Melle Mel that he isn't the meanest to grab the mic. Even MC Lyte had to declare herself the best to do it. Some call it cocky or arrogant, but many of us can embrace a healthy confidence in our lives to motivate ourselves to dream astronomically.

There isn't room for mediocre thinking when you're taking over the world. "I'm just okay" won't cut through barriers, glass ceilings, or tough industry standards. We will always lose when we undervalue ourselves. Don't enough people already do that for us?

When asked why he named his album *G.O.A.T.*, LL responded in an interview with Barnesandnoble.com, "'cause it was better than naming it *LL Is a Pretty Good Rapper*." Who can argue with that? Maybe I'll name my next book *G.O.A.T.* and see where that gets me. But for right now, I'll just stick to the facts: I'm one bad mofo.

25. Respect the Architect

ARTIST: GURU, FEATURING BAHAMADIA AND RAMSEY LEWIS
ALBUM: JAZZMATAZZ, VOLUME II: THE NEW REALITY (1995)

THE FIRST RULE to becoming a great writer is to read. Everything. Especially exceptional writers. Those who do what you want to do and do it well. The reasoning is multilayered. By studying your predecessors, you'll start to develop your style. But also in reading creative geniuses you'll gain respect for the craft and the greats before you who made it seem effortless.

When I dip into the works of architects like James Baldwin, after I get over my initial intimidation, I'm always awed by what can be done with words. Baldwin was equally creative and eloquent. He and other brilliant writers motivate me to push my own creative boundaries and strive for greatness.

There's continuous dismay in hip-hop circles about the lack of respect old-school MCs receive from a new crop of rappers—which has been going on almost since there was such a thing as an MC. Case in point: Remember how hot Diddy was when members of Da Band from *Making the Band 2* didn't know the words to Sugarhill Gang's "Rapper's Delight," the first commercially successful rap song? There was a good reason why he made them learn it: if you don't know where you're from, how can you possibly know where you're going?

Through his *Jazzmatazz* series, Guru, one-half of the groundbreaking hip-hop group Gang Starr, helped to successfully illustrate the marriage between jazz and hip-hop—a merging of old-school with new-school. "Respect the Architect," which features one of the more underrated MCs, Bahamadia, brings in pianist and jazz legend Ramsey Lewis, who's been rocking audiences since the '50s, to demonstrate the importance of appreciating antecedent musical greats. A classic line from old-school hip-hopper Biz Markie that repeats the title of the song is scratched in. Another merging of the old with the new.

Hip-hop isn't the only subculture that suffers from a lack of historical understanding. For the most part, people have faulty memories and short attention spans, especially as it relates to folks who aren't in our current eyeshot. We are quick to forget about originators and quicker to assume the roles of both Alpha and Omega. Knowing our history, especially as it relates to our ambitions, can jolt us with confidence, provide priceless insight, and encourage us to be better.

I'm far from reading everyone who I should read. It's overwhelming to think about all the books that I need to ingest, all the writers I should know. But I'm grateful that so many geniuses left behind their works for me to consume, study, and learn from. They've allowed me to stand on their shoulders to peek into my own career. Thanks, James.

26. Don't Let It Go to Your Head

ARTIST: BRAND NUBIAN
ALBUM: FOUNDATION (1998)

IN COLLEGE MY homeboy used to call me Big Head. It was a term of endearment. I don't really have a big head. At least I don't think. I mean I do have my father's forehead, which protrudes slightly. Okay, not the point. My friend and I could joke like that, but even if my dome is a little large for my body, I don't ever want to suffer from the real cranium threat, bigheadedness.

On the album *Foundation*, Brand Nubian, known for keeping it gutter and provocative, tackles fundamental subjects of life. So it's appropriate for them to explore bigheadedness, the disorder that makes us ego-trip. With a soulful hook, courtesy of a sample from a song with the same title, "Don't Let It Go to Your Head" is a warning against catching what countless numbers of people have already contracted.

Humility isn't like blood in that we're born with it circulating through our bodies. As humans, with innate desires to be recognized, we are especially susceptible to acquiring a big head when we've achieved some sort of success.

There are all kinds of "triggers" that can make us inflate into big-headedness. Common ones include:

- A new relationship: you can't hang with your homegirl anymore, because she's "taken" and the mere act of being near you may make her catch the single disease again.
- Winning something/anything: Uncle Cleo won a thousand dollars in a lottery scratch-off, and all of a sudden he acts like he doesn't know you.
- Moving to a better neighborhood: now you're George Jefferson because you've changed zip codes.
- New job: now you're someone with a better title.
- Penning a best-selling book: encourage your friends to buy this book, and I'll prove that I won't change.
- Recording deal: I'm sure we all know someone who's going to be a star and already acts like a celebrity.
- Cameo in a music video: just because the camera pans by her for two seconds, she thinks she's famous.
- Change tax brackets: pick a rapper who's come into penthouse money.

This is just a sampling. But I would like to think that we can physically feel when our head expands. If not, however, here are some symptoms of bigheadedness:

- A stank attitude toward anyone who you perceive is not on your level.
- Spending an inordinate amount of time thinking about yourself.
- Surrounding yourself with people who frequently pump up your head on cue.

Let's not confuse bigheadedness with confidence. It's healthy to be proud of our successes or good fortunes. And let us not charge humility with being weak. Modesty does not make one soft.

Bigheadedness is dangerous because, as Brand Nubian warned, one minute you can be on top, and the next you can't even be on *The Surreal Life*. Everyone you alienated during your illness has written you off like a bad check. Now you're alone. Your big head can't even comfort you. It deflated.

Being humble is a conscious act that requires a solid grounding and the understanding that our success isn't achieved in a bubble. We all like to believe that when we "blow up" we'll remember the little people and retain our around-the-way, down-for-the-cause status. We'll always be real. But many of us come into good fortune before we even know who we are. So it's important to keep that head in check and monitor early warning signs. No matter what angle you look at it, bigheadedness is never cute.

27. Treat 'Em Right

ARTIST: CHUBB ROCK
ALBUM: THE ONE (1991)

THERE'S NOTHING WORSE than ungrateful celebrities. You know, the kind who don't want to sign autographs for fans, or who have acquired amnesia regarding all the people who helped to establish their career. They suffer from extreme cases of bigheadedness. I hate to hear about a celebrity who I admire, respect, support, and paid to see turn out to be an arrogant ass. Leaves a Robitussin taste in my mouth. Without the grounds people buying CDs, movie tickets, clothes, or books, celebrities would still be working that crappy before-I-made-it-big job.

In the early '90s, when Brooklyn-representing rapper Chubb Rock was experiencing some success, he released "Treat 'Em Right," which reflects on the importance of giving back to fans. There's one line in the song where he mentions that he always signs autographs. I remember thinking at the time that if I ever ran into the Chubbster, I would ensure that he would keep his promise. I never had the opportunity (no, I wouldn't bumrush Chubb if I saw him today), but it was nice to hear a rapper acknowledging the folks who help to feed him.

I've found that it's not just celebrities who forget about the little people. I've helped friends to write essays, letters, and business plans, and to find jobs, apartments, and mates, and in the end my assistance wasn't even acknowledged. No utterance of "thank you." Noted.

This is what happens when we're ungrateful. People start to question our humility. I know we get busy, become caught up, and sometimes forget to offer our gratitude. I've fallen victim to the professional distractions that constantly take us away from what's important. But these are still weak excuses. Even if we aren't in the position where millions of people have contributed to our success, we can't forget about the ten, twenty, or even hundred who have.

I don't want to be on anyone's "Ungrateful Mofo" list, so I try to make sure that at the least I say the two words that are more powerful than we like to recognize. Quite often when people help us, they're not always expecting reciprocation of the favor. They usually just want acknowledgment of their actions.

There have been countless indispensable individuals who have pushed me along. They comprise my "Down from Day One" list. While I still try to find my way, "thank you" remains free and painless. A combination I can always get with.

28. It Takes Two

ARTIST: ROB BASE & DJ E-Z ROCK
ALBUM: IT TAKES TWO (1988)

THERE WAS A time in hip-hop when the DJ was the main attraction and the MC was merely on stage as a hype-man. This was even years before a Long Island MC proclaimed that DJ Eric B. was president. The fact was evident: hip-hop was not a one-cat show. The DJ needed the MC, and the MC damn sure needed the DJ.

The prioritized role of the DJ has diminished, and songs like "Me Against the World," "Sole Survivor," and "Do It Myself" imply a solo mission despite the fact that hip-hop is a crew-oriented culture.

"It Takes Two" is a supreme party song. Anytime it's played in a mix, you want to throw an impromptu backyard barbeque and initiate a *Soul Train* line. Just thinking about the thumping track makes me want to break out into a quick Running Man.

Following protocol to name check the DJ, Rob Base shout-outs E-Z Rock a few times in "It Takes Two" and also falls back to give his partner the last segment of the song to "get busy" scratching. The bond between MC and DJ is a give-and-take.

It's truly the hook, which repeats the song's title, that resonates in my adult life. It definitely "takes two to make a thing go right." If you want to get deep, the song implies a powerful statement about the miracle of life. There's a reason why we can't create life alone. The journey is not supposed to be traveled solo. Life is not a one-cat show.

I'm not in a hip-hop group, but I have a DJ. My best friend Sai doesn't spin or scratch, but she backs me up. We rode bikes together, applied to grad school together, and fought the battles of life together. Whenever I'm performing in my life's stage show, *Black Girl Dreams*—taking on a new project, following my ambition up and down the East Coast, or writing a book—she's there to remind me that I'm not alone. She hypes me to crowds and tells them I'm the greatest thing to come along since George Foreman grills. And when it's her time to perform, I do the same. No matter how far away we may live, or how busy we become, we always represent for one another.

Many of us have that one person who always has our back, front, and side. Road dawg. Partner-in-crime. Bonnie or Clyde. This relationship deserves special attention and is one that shouldn't be taken for granted. Next time you're performing, don't forget to name drop your DJ.

Sai and I have been battling the world together for more than twenty years and we continue to support one another in our endeavors. We're truly a dynamic duo. Unstoppable. Life takes two.

29. Karma

ARTIST: BLACK EYED PEAS
ALBUM: BEHIND THE FRONT (1998)

YEARS AGO, WHEN I used to write poetry, or rather put together short lines of words that rhymed, I penned a little ditty about using my girl Karma to handle all my dirty work. It was inspired by a dude who did me wrong. The "poem" was quite silly, actually. It compared karma to a superhero and told my troubled amour that I didn't have to key his car, burn his clothes, or flatten his tires. I thought it was clever at the time. Note: I have not actually ever keyed a car or burned clothes. Or at least as of yet I haven't been appropriately provoked. Just kidding?

Although my rhyme didn't accurately explain how karma works, the underlying message of it and of the Black Eyed Peas's "Karma" is that our actions operate on a cause-and-effect model. Over a groovy track, one that makes you want to two-step with a reggae twist, the group impersonates karma to show its omniscient power and confirm that "ain't no running" from it. Three hundred and sixty degrees.

Remember when we were younger? Karma was our parents, who

dished out the punishments for our ill-advised actions. As adults, without Moms and Pops there holding the belt, we sometimes forget that our actions are still governed by a higher power. Many times, the effects of karma aren't immediate and won't be waiting for us at the door like our parents used to do if we were late for curfew. So we tend to believe that our actions go unnoticed, without consequence.

A friend of mine told me that he didn't believe in karma. My response: *Does it matter if you do or not?* He tried to justify his wrongdoings and convince himself that no repercussions would result. I wished him luck.

Thankfully, I have an incredibly guilty conscience that usually dictates my actions. And a sensitive stomach (Pepto-Bismol stays in my purse) that can't handle the grumbling pain that comes along with committing an act that I know is straight-up foul. Plus I've seen karma perform in my own life, and I'm still reeling from my boomeranged actions.

This isn't to advertise that we should act as decent human beings with some moral framework only because we fear retaliation, similar to big conglomerates that "give" to the community to recover from a public humiliation. We should do so because, well, it's the right thing to do. I know, very Huxtable. But when we get into a pattern of letting our actions release positive energy, it becomes natural.

On the flipside, when someone does us wrong, we want to seek the sweet revenge 2Pac once mused about. As much as I'm tempted to call on the Black Hoodies, doing so blemishes my karma. Not worth it. So as I

implied in my corny rhyme, I feel fairly confident knowing that people who have done me dirty generate my revenge. I don't have to lift a finger or my voice. I focus my energy on creating positive abundance in my life. There's no better retribution than outshining enemies.

30. *Everything Is Everything*

ARTIST: LAURYN HILL
ALBUM: THE MISEDUCATION OF LAURYN HILL (1998)

I WAS HAVING what I call a pissy-elevator day. From the moment my apartment door slammed behind me, everything started out bad. I reached the elevator of my Harlem high-rise complex (not to be mistaken for George Jefferson's sky-rise), and the putrid odor of urine invaded my senses. I would have to ride down seventeen flights smelling someone's waste. Not to mention that I was struggling with a recent breakup and the stress of making ends meet in a freelance career. An older woman, who got on around the thirteenth floor, and carried more bags than she could manage and had fewer teeth than she deserved, asked me how I was doing as we traveled in the smelly elevator together. I answered perfunctorily, "Fine." To which she replied, "Everything is going to be all right. It may feel like the end of the world, but you have to be thankful for each day that you are living above the ground. Things will turn around." Her words were a sucker punch to my conscience. Poignant. Clairvoyant. Perfectly timed. A profound power was speaking through her. She gave me chills.

Although I pump my fist in the air about seizing one's destiny, the individual's role in making things happen, and having a map in place to reach your potential, I can't dismiss the role of the Master Plan. The Creator's predestined direction for our life, where all the pieces fit like my niece's puzzle.

Lauryn Hill's "Everything Is Everything" could be the choir's selection at church on Sunday. Similar to her soul godfather Sam Cooke, Hill releases from the heart a hip-hop spiritual where "change, it comes eventually." She sings about self-love as a solution to failure, dedication to our harvest, where we reap what we sow, and how even when it seems like our dreams won't ever materialize, we must maintain our faith.

Like the next hip-hopper, I've suffered my share of disappointments. Not being chosen for gigs that I thought I was perfect for. Failed relationships with men who I thought would make great partners. Not achieving a financial breakthrough although I've been working my butt off. Often I've handled these disappointments incorrectly. I fret, sulk, and wonder why, why, why! I waste time envisioning the possibilities. I start my day with a frown.

Lately, however, I've been handling these breaks of life with much more poise and understanding. More specifically, I fall back and let God do what He does. Faith and trust become best friends who rub my back and dry my tears.

You've probably heard the saying, "If you want to make God laugh, tell him about your plans." Falling back reduces the pang of disappointment, because you don't focus on the rejection. You focus on the potential of God's bigger and better alternative. A better job. A better mate. A better house. A better situation. A better life.

I still have pissy-elevator days, but I open my eyes to see all the signs around me that tell me, as Lauryn Hill sang, "after winter, must come spring."

31. *Ghetto Bastard* (Everything's Gonna be Alright)

ARTIST: NAUGHTY BY NATURE
ALBUM: NAUGHTY BY NATURE (1991)

WHY ME? HAVE you ever asked yourself this question to explain your reality? Sometimes it seems like our destiny is predetermined from the moment we exit the womb. Genetics, melanin, and the number of parents present in the delivery room seem to decide the course of our lives.

"Ghetto Bastard" is an angry account from Naughty by Nature's Treach about being born into a world where the sun doesn't shine and his mother can't afford to take care of him. The song begins in the hospital, where a doctor declares the fatherless child a member of the "born losers" and contributor to a societal "problem." The infant is judged before he can talk. His success in life is already concluded by outsiders. The hook, however, is straight from the silver-lining train of thought that "everything's gonna be alright."

I used to think that some eternal optimistic arguments were too simplistic, a shallow attempt to provide a solution to a complex predicament. Then I realized that I just have a problem with the language. When we hear troubled two-word mandates like "ghetto bastard," "African orphan," "child slave," and "crack baby," the phrase "everything will work out" doesn't seem to capture the necessary magnitude of hope. The words, which don't seem to be backed by a powerful force of change, don't seem strong enough to visualize a different reality.

So we ask, *Why me?* We spend significant time dwelling on the question, not necessarily seeking an answer, but as a way to sympathize with our own situations. We fall into the position that we've been assigned instead of the role that we're supposed to play. We become angry. We fight ourselves. And we look at faith as empty rhetoric.

When we enter this world, we're already endowed with an abundance of hope, potent enough to sustain us. So if the words "everything is going to be alright" aren't vast enough to describe the strength within us, we can concentrate on feeling it.

In my life, I don't have it one-quarter as bad as my little brothers and sisters in Africa. Or my little brothers and sisters in Baltimore. And I'm always amazed at those who are smaller than me who yield twice my strength and hope. We're all prefilled with the power we need to survive. Can you feel it?

32. Jesus Walks

ARTIST: KANYE WEST
ALBUM: THE COLLEGE DROPOUT (2004)

LIKE MANY HIP-HOPPERS, I was raised in the church. I woke up every Sunday morning as a toddler, young girl, and teenager and put on my best dress clothes to go to service. The older I got, the more I battled my mother about going. Sometimes I played sick. Other times, I faked exhaustion, which didn't really work that well. More often than not, I rolled to church upset, wishing I could be in my bed chilling under the covers. Now, as I wrestle with adulthood, I'm fighting to go back.

My youth allowed me to slide without having to address being a product of both hip-hop and the church. As an adult, though, I've struggled to reconcile the spiritual grounding from my upbringing with the culture that's embedded within me. How is it that I can shake what Momma gave me to hypnotic beats and sleezy rhymes on Saturday night and wake up Sunday morning with a hangover, only to find myself praying along with Dr. Creflo Dollar as I attend his televised service from the comfort of my sofa?

Kanye West's "Jesus Walks," cowritten with fellow Chi-town rapper Rhymefest, demonstrates the sometimes-thorny relationship between hip-hoppers and spirituality. Doesn't God love all of his children, including the strippers and the rap music lovers, as West asserts?

Before West contemplated whether or not his record would be played on the radio because he rhymed about Jesus, a thread of spirituality had been running in hip-hop for decades. And for good reason. We all need peace from the madness surrounding us. It's why some rappers thank God even though they seem to worship the holy trinity of chicks, cash, and crack. It's why former stick-up kid DMX includes prayers on his albums, and why Allah is heavily name-dropped on tracks. We have our own Reverend Run and have witnessed the emergence of hip-hop churches under the guidance of legendary rapper Kurtis Blow.

Granted, it seems contradictory to rhyme about slingin' one minute and switch to praying the next, but I currently reside in a glass house and am not in a position to assess how far other hip-hoppers are from "righteousness" or evaluate how they express their beliefs. I have my own to resolve. The more I learn about the world, the more I know I can't make it through the valley by myself. Lawd help me!

The process of reconciliation and finding one's balance is an extension of maturity and spiritual-based growth. After much reflection, I've realized that I can be hip-hop and have a relationship with God. Hip-hop, popular culture, or any outside force, for that matter, shouldn't dictate my actions or my thoughts; I have the power to decide what aspects I choose to embrace. And as I continue to develop spiritually, I want to hug those elements that heighten my consciousness and strengthen my faith, not destroy them.

I know that I am able to write this book because God flows through me. He's given me the tools to accomplish such a feat. I know that I rise every morning because of Him. And I'm grateful for His mercy, because a sista messes up.

Shall I testify?

While I believe a bridge is being built between popular culture and spirituality, it's about finding the balance right for you, which, like life, is arduous and continuous. As my person grows, I understand the roles these two forces play in my life, and I work to make them interact harmoniously, like a Lauryn Hill album.

Our imperfections and contradictions shouldn't stop us from acknowledging, developing, and embracing our divine selves. They should motivate us to change for the better. There is room for spirituality in our grayish, hip-hop lives.

Word and Amen.

33. Faithful

ARTIST: COMMON, FEATURING BILAL AND JOHN LEGEND
ALBUM: BE (2005)

AS A LITTLE girl, no more than six or seven years old, I used to sit at the top of the carpeted steps in my house, peering through the bars and watching my mother as she prayed in the living room. It had to be 6:00 a.m. Every morning this was her routine. Every morning this was my routine. I sat quietly. I don't think she ever knew I was sitting there, watching. I don't know what she was praying for. But a few years later when she packed her two children up and moved to Baltimore, alone, without a job, there was a reason for prayer.

"God moves," Common says before he begins rhyming in his song "Faithful." Known for lacing his art with spirituality, the Chi-town MC personifies God as a woman, as he once did with hip-hop, and attempts to answer the questions: How would he treat God if she were his woman? Would he remain faithful? If God were his woman, he ponders, would he continue to want his ex-partners: lies, greed, drugs, and sex?

In his second verse he explores faith in humanity by relating the tale of a married man who's tested by other women. Does he remain faithful to his wife? To himself? In less than five minutes Common simultaneously invokes the trials of spiritual faith and human trust and implies that there's no difference. Soul cats Bilal and John Legend belt out that we should be "faithful to the end." And you believe.

I've never doubted my mother. My faith in her is unshakeable. When I was a little girl and she would tell me, "Everything will be all right," those were the only words I needed to hear to have a good night's sleep.

So I wonder why I can't have that same resolute faith in the corners of my life. If God were a woman, if God were my mother, wouldn't I trust her just the same? I trust the woman that God moves through, my mother. Don't I trust that He moves in my life, too?

For me, the concept of faith is both liberating and demanding. The act of letting go and placing my worries and concerns into the hands of God is freedom. But, it requires a sophisticated faith, and sometimes I wonder if I can trust enough.

As Common so eloquently points out, we exercise faith in different manifestations every day. Each time we walk out of the house and expect to return, we're faithful. Every day, without realizing it, we reside in hope.

To this day, I like to replay the scene in my mind of my mother in the living room. It's faith in action. And I trust, God moves through that woman and through this daughter.

34. The Truth

ARTIST: PHAROAHE MONCH, FEATURING COMMON AND TALIB KWELI
ALBUM: INTERNAL AFFAIRS (1999)

IN HIGH SCHOOL I took a class called Truth of Knowledge, which aimed to dissect the tenets of truth and prompt critical analysis of fact versus belief. I know, you're probably thinking exactly what I was thinking at the time, *Huh?* During our class discussions, we talked in circles to reveal that people of all ages have strong inclinations to bend the truth and to avoid it like homework assignments. I was fifteen years old, and all the course did was give me a revolving headache, a knack for empty rhetoric, and a crooked eye toward the words coming out of my boyfriend's mouth.

Years later the subject remains just as simple and complex as illuminated in "The Truth," a reflective song by three MCs with conscious thoughts. Produced by crate digger Diamond, the track features an assembly of strings, the softness of a woman's vocals, and random piano notes, which collectively establish a meditative sound. Pharoahe Monch rhymes in his disjointed style about the lies we tell ourselves, the false truths that are usually far more potent than the ones we tell others. The deep-rooted Common spits about recognizing truth in humanity and not in institutions. Talib Kweli foreshadows how the truth is a driver for freedom. It was rhymed: the truth should be sought internally, externally, and with diligence. So why do we avoid it like tax day, cover it up like burkas, or manipulate it like an image in Photoshop?

We live in a society that accepts gradients of fact and placebos of truth, because they go down easier. Politicians lie like it's a job prerequisite. We lie to our loved ones as if they're our enemies. A friend once told me that he tells women he dates partial truths, because they can't handle the full version. That was a lame excuse. My response was, "They can handle the truth. They just won't handle it the way you want them to." He knows that lying is a much easier task, like putting dishes in the dishwasher only to find out they're still dirty. Lies become affixed to your conscience just like food particles stuck to plates.

"Everyone's truth is different, but there's only one truth," Pharoahe Monch told me to explain the impetus behind his song, which he considers one of the deeper ones in his musical catalog. Hip-hop culture was groomed to speak truth to the masses, but at some point we forgot that we have to first speak that truth to ourselves. Maybe the truth is that you really do have a drinking problem. Maybe the truth is that you do prefer a mate of the same sex. Maybe the truth is that you are a victim of domestic violence. Maybe, as Pharoahe Monch mused, the truth is that you are ugly on the inside.

The famous hip-hop credo "respect mine" should mean respect one's truth. The lies we live undermine our potential. Suffocating the truth cuts off our air supply. Avoidance is killing us softly. Its accomplices—

shame, guilt, and denial—change us into someone else. We can't control the lies that others tell us (although we can decipher and reject them), so it is doubly important for us to banish the lies that we tell ourselves.

In my relatively short life, I've had to face my share of truth and confront the beautiful and sometimes troubled being that I am, the beautiful and sometimes troubled beings who surround me, and the beautiful and sometimes troubled world that I live in. It hurts sometimes when I think about my reality, but I find the cloth of humanity soothing. It becomes easier to be honest with myself and with others; it becomes easier to deal with the truth of others and our world. Eventually, truth becomes freedom.

Politics
as
Usual

PART THREE

35. Things Done Changed

ARTIST: THE NOTORIOUS B.I.G.
ALBUM: READY TO DIE (1994)

MY MOTHER GREW up on a street in Baltimore that now I would be nervous to ride down in broad daylight. Crime has killed the neighborhood watch. But the memories of her block are of a place where neighbors could leave their doors unlocked. There wasn't fear of break-ins. She could walk the streets and not worry about anyone messing with her, because folks around the way respected her father. Children didn't act a fool in or out of their parent's presence, because a neighbor was sure to relay any news of bad behavior. The last time my mother and I rode down her street, it was a block filled with boarded-up houses. A thick smog of abandonment hung in the air. What happened?

In "Things Done Changed" Biggie didn't pinpoint a specific moment, but he pondered the same issue. When did his neighborhood transform from a place simmering with smokin' summer barbeques to a battlefield where childhood friends get smoked? The parents who watched their children grow, he roared, are now scared of them. What happened?

The reasoning is complex, horrifying, and institutional. But as much as Civil Rights progression may have marched backward, we've seen some advancement from the days of segregated bathrooms. For one, we didn't have this thing called hip-hop and the limitless possibility to exploit its power to revolutionize our communities.

Biggie was right. Things are different. The hope in me wants to believe that society has changed in both directions. We can fall victim to the worst of the times, or we can elevate with the best of the times. Biggie raged about the limited career possibilities for folks in his neighborhood: pushing dope, playing hoops, and the new option for which he was grateful, writing rhymes. But isn't it up to us to expand these options for ourselves? Aren't we familiar with creating opportunity out of chaos?

Things may worsen. Things may get better. But in between the ranges of our conditions, we remain our most powerful weapons. We have to adapt to our changing environments and find productive ways to compete, challenge, and take charge. We need to use us. Our survival depends on it.

36. *Why*

ARTIST: JADAKISS
ALBUM: KISS OF DEATH (2004)

MY NIECE IS at that inquisitive stage where the question "Why?" follows every statement. I'll say, "Don't pull on that." She'll ask, "Why?" I'll tell her that she might hurt herself. And she returns with, "Why?" I have to admit that after about the fourth "why," she's worked my nerves. But how can I be annoyed by her learning about the world around her? Especially when I've realized that as adults, we tend to abandon our sense of inquiry. We don't ask "why" enough.

I remember calling my boy to ask him had he heard the new Jadakiss joint, aptly called "Why." I was a fan of the D-Block member's lyrical ability, but wanted to hear the Yonkers-bred rapper expand his subject matter beyond guns and clips. "Why" was the fresh direction that became one of his more successfully commercial tracks. Forget what you heard, hip-hop fans do welcome political art.

The song is a series of "whys" tackling a myriad of puzzling topics like 9/11, the deaths of 2Pac and the Notorious B.I.G., a cure for AIDS, the politics of rap music, and why folks are more concerned with looking fly than stacking dough.

Ironically enough, some radio and television stations deemed "Why" so provocative that they bleeped out the word "Bush" as it was associated with the Twin Towers. MTV, a network known for booty-shaking bliss, played an edited version of the video. The song was eventually banned on some outlets, and the empty talking head Bill O'Reilly called Jadakiss a "smear merchant." Jadakiss told the Associated Press, "As a rapper, as an artist, we've got power. . . . In the beginning, they would edit [the song], but after that, everybody called back for the version that was calling Bush [out]."

Of course we wanted to hear the original song. Jadakiss was raising questions that many of us wanted to ask. An edited version meant our voices were abbreviated. Why?

Sometimes I wonder where we would be if people didn't inquire about our ugly realities. What if African Americans didn't question "equality"? What if activists didn't question apartheid in South Africa? In history, the three-lettered question has been a catalyst for change. The search for an explanation provokes action.

The "why" can also be simple and personal. I used to say "I'm broke" so often that I got tired of hearing myself state the obvious. So I switched it up and asked myself *why* I was so broke and began looking for solutions to improve my situation. One answer was right in front of my face—stop buying crap!

The moment we stop to ask "why," we put ourselves in a vulnerable position of complacency and ignorance. We leave important questions unanswered. We accept things we may not understand. We relinquish our power to change our situations.

I can only encourage my niece's queries, because with each one she expands her understanding of the world around her. Her questioning may spark a revolution. In the meantime, we should all ask the simple and hard "whys" so that our younger selves will grow up and do the same.

37. *Parents Just Don't Understand*

ARTIST: D.J. JAZZY JEFF AND THE FRESH PRINCE
ALBUM: HE'S THE DJ, I'M THE RAPPER (1988)

CONFESSION TIME. I played my "Parents Just Don't Understand" record so much you would have thought I was receiving a check for each spin. I knew all the cute, elementary lyrics like I was the third member of the Philly duo. If you throw the song on today, I will do the wop until my arms hurt.

"Parents Just Don't Understand" was one of the more harmless songs that I included in my adolescent anthem collection. Through his comical narrative ripped from the day of the life of any teenager, Fresh Prince voiced my angst: the infamous school clothes debacle; the dilemma of how much trouble you should get into when your parents go out of town, which is directly proportionate to how much punishment you're willing to risk; and the unraveling of stupidity when you get caught doing something you have no business doing. The video, seemingly produced on a dollar-store budget, was equally as colorful. Fresh Prince showcased his early acting skills through scene-by-scene performances of the song's storyline.

As a young person, it seemed that adults didn't take the time to truly understand me or my plight. And of course because I was usually wrapped up in my social turmoil of the day, I couldn't care less about theirs. My mother and all other adults knew best, and I knew it all.

While the parent/child tug-of-war is expected, "Parents Just Don't Understand" two-steps toward a bigger generational gap between adults and young people that threatens to undermine our collective bargaining. Depression babies didn't understand why their children wanted to twist and shout. Civil Righters who marched for freedom didn't understand hip-hoppers who breakdanced for liberation. The tagging hip-hop generation isn't sure how to connect with the youngsters who swear by the "Chicken Noodle Soup" dance. And no one is really communicating.

On a dreary afternoon while I was living in Boston, I headed to the "T," Beantown's subway, and stood in line to buy tokens from an older black gentleman. While counting my money, he pointed to my white headphones that I never left home without and asked me what I was listening to. When I replied "hip-hop" with a smile, he launched into a "Rap Is Worthless" campaign. His soapbox speech, given from behind glass and through an intercom, lasted fifteen seconds too long. I had heard it all before. Therefore, I was two seconds away from blowing up his three-by-three spot accordingly: *First of all, you don't know me. You don't know what I'm listening to. Not all hip-hop music deserves to be condemned to hell. In fact, there is plenty that is good, if not damn motivational. Here you are behind the counter selling me subway tokens, and I'm on my way to an event for graduate school. And you're saying that hip-hop messed me up?*

Frustration boiled and young arrogance emerged. But I didn't explode. Luckily, Momma ain't raised no fool. She embedded in me the old-school value of respecting one's elders (within reason, of course—like I said, Momma ain't raise no fool). My mental tirade reflected the buildup of the many Civil Righters who judged me because of the generation I was born into, which in turn judged my person, my friends, my lifestyle, and my perspective. Subway Pops offended me. Underground, in front of that station booth, the complex generational divide widened.

Yet, one offense doesn't necessarily warrant another. Truth is, just being who he is, a Civil Righter, he's helped to make it possible for me to attend graduate school by acting as a buffer for the blunt end of racism. Although he was quick to brush off my hip-hop self as trivial, it wasn't right for me to do the same.

As I sat on the train after dealing with Subway Pops, my emotions and logic began to collide. A group of loud teens boarded and interrupted my inner reflection. My generational prejudice crept up. My face scowled at the young girls who wore suffocating t-shirts and the boys who were swallowed in theirs. They talked at microphone levels like they were auditioning for a *Menace II Society* reality show. Now who was judging whom? I had to check myself quick.

Sometimes different age groups just don't understand one another. More often, we simply forget. Did I not broadcast my business at an earth-shattering volume as I walked the aisles of the local mall, wearing clothes just as tacky, caught up in my perfect storm of attention-seeking adolescence? Didn't my mother complain that my shirt was too tight or my skirt was too short? As much as things change, they remain the same.

Holding on to judgmental attitudes is risky no matter what end of the hill we're standing on. Assuming that a person can't understand you because of his or her age, or vice versa, is no way to spark a much-needed discussion to build bridges of understanding. Every generation needs to know when to fall back, listen, and learn.

Although Subway Pops caught me off guard, I should have used our time to dialogue. I should have exposed him to the breadth of hip-hop music. I should have explained to him that hip-hop hasn't messed me up, nor will I let it. I should have asked him why he had such negative feelings about the culture that I love. We should have communicated. And I could have had a similar conversation with my younger selves on the train. They are me, and I was them. I can understand.

Now a member of the sacred parenthood, Will Smith, who dropped the "Fresh Prince" moniker years ago (hip-hop can look good grown, can't it?), would probably rhyme a different tune to his children: adults can understand, sometimes they do know what's best, and your perspective is important.

38. Ladies First

ARTIST: QUEEN LATIFAH, FEATURING MONIE LOVE
ALBUM: ALL HAIL THE QUEEN (1989)

I WAS A fourth-grader when I got the genius idea to dress up like Santa Claus for Halloween. My mother copped me a costume from Woolworth's. I had never seen anyone in my school dress up as the cheery gift-giver before. This was going to be monumental. Picture me, a brown girl with a long white beard, a pillow around my waist, and my best *ho, ho, ho* (catch the irony?). My jolliness was immediately interrupted when the class ass, a white kid with dusty blond hair and a parade of freckles on his face, shouted during the middle of lunchtime: "You can't be Santa Claus, because you're a girl and you're black." The lunch table became silent. I turned black girl on him, put my finger in his face, and said, "I can be whatever I want to be." A collective moan overtook my classmates—98 percent of them were white—as I walked away.

Two minutes later, I was crying in the girls' bathroom. My rosy cheeks washed away with my tears. I wasn't upset at the fact that he called me out for being black and female. That's a beautiful fact. I was mad that he thought he had the power to tell me what I could and couldn't do.

Right around the time of the Santa Claus incident, Queen Latifah had the audacity to release a feminist hip-hop tribute called "Ladies First." When I saw the Queen on television rocking a goddess hat, fully clothed, and rhyming, I was mesmerized. She looked royal. "Ladies First" also features British-born raptress Monie Love, who told me that Latifah had the concept to do a song that would uplift women. Monie Love remembered meeting Latifah in England in early '88, when Latifah was the only female on the road with three male acts. The two ladies hit it off and went on to record a song that was, in Monie's words, about "unity, pride, and skill amongst women."

In nearly all aspects of hip-hop culture, females had to continuously prove their worth to be down. Young women had to prove they were tough enough to spin on their heads. Tough enough to climb fences to tag subway cars. Tough enough to bring it at the Latin Quarter. Tough enough to be the editor in chief of a hip-hop magazine. Tough enough to write a book about hip-hop. Tough enough to challenge hip-hop. But these blockades didn't stop fearless femmes from kicking in the door and announcing their presence. By exercising her voice through the art of rhyme, Dana Owens, aka Queen Latifah, practiced the best in feminism.

My mother told me that when she was ready to enter the workforce in the '60s there were three career options for women (that is, if you weren't a stay-at-home wife): nurse, social worker, or teacher. Oh, hell no. Those alternatives wouldn't have worked for me. I'm grateful to the ladies who preceded me and expanded my options.

Hip-hop is reflective of our larger society, where sexism, albeit more covert than older versions, still lurks. For females, the very act of pursuing their dreams and desires, even for an aspiration like dressing up as Santa Claus for Halloween, can be groundbreaking and barrier shattering. Gender shouldn't stop anyone from following her heart.

When I see the Queen now receive an Academy Award nomination, represent lovely on cosmetic commercials, or release a jazz album, she doesn't have to say one word. I already know.

Ladies first.

39. Turn Off the Radio

ARTIST: ICE CUBE
ALBUM: AMERIKKKA'S MOST WANTED (1990)

I **CAN'T LIVE** or work without music. Even when I toiled in corporate America, I found inventive ways to bring CDs and headphones to keep me sane in my cubicle. Now that my office is a studio apartment the size of Mariah Carey's closet, I'm like Radio Raheem in *Do the Right Thing*–I blast my motivation.

Call it research, pure laziness, or just self-inflicted psychological pain, but on one snowy workday I spent a good half of it listening to a premier urban radio station, which I've decided to call WACK-FM: Hot 5 Hits.

In just one afternoon I heard enough Beyoncé to make me lose my mind to the point that I wanted to pack up everything I owned and bolt to a land free of the Houston diva. My ears were clogged with so much Lil Jon and his troop of wannabes that I wanted to snap my fingers and transport myself to a place where I'm not told how to dance. If I heard another unintelligible ode to a luxury car, I was tempted to throw some Ds (rims) at the freakin' radio. Then there were the guys in the boy bands who I wanted to take over my knee like Big Momma, because they were too young to croon about their sexual appetites. Oh and yes, Jay-Z,

I know that thirty is the new twenty and that sometimes we lose one even if I show you what I got. But damn, can I get a rest, Jigga? The same five songs were regurgitated every half hour, and even when I switched to another station, to paraphrase hip-hop group Digital Underground, all around the radio, same song.

In less than three minutes "Turn Off the Radio" is a furious charge to stations that ignored hip-hop, opting for softer R&B and Top 40 hits, a decision that was part moral, part fear-induced, and part uncertainty. Coming from a godfather of gangsta music, it's ironic that one of the accusations against radio today is that it's too street. It's not surprising that several years later, after Cube's radio indictment, dead prez—the self-proclaimed, revolutionary gangstas who project Cube's resentment, but with a Panther's agenda—would release a song and two mixtapes called "Turn Off the Radio."

What makes the stakes high is that the current monotonous state of urban radio can be deemed intentional. Between payola, the pay-for-play movement where radio executives and DJs receive dough and gifts to keep certain music in heavy rotation, and consolidation, where Clear Channel, a corporate behemoth, has grown from approximately forty stations to owning more than eleven hundred, it's you and me, average listeners, who lose out while we subconsciously nod our heads and relinquish our entertainment rights.

This narrowing of choices isn't just decaying radio. I hear people declare all the time that there aren't any good books published, and television has morphed into a reality-show wasteland. All of these arguments may be valid, but what are we going to do about it?

We have more control than we'd like to admit. Instead of complaining to ourselves, let's turn off the radio, petition our local stations, seek alternatives, and become active participants in our media consumption.

There's an entire world outside of mainstream radio, BET, and Fox News. Real head-nodding hip-hop music is alive and well, although your favorite radio DJ may not put you on to it. Also, the Internet is home to alternative and independent media that is worthy of being embraced.

There's always the option of creating our own media (sound familiar, hip-hoppers?) in a range of platforms—magazines, television programs, movies, music, and books. What better way to control the images and information we ingest than to create them ourselves?

With all the media that hits us on a daily basis, it deserves to be balanced. Since when is eating a diet consisting only of fatty foods a good idea? If you're really gangsta, you could fast until your favorite hip-hop station plays an Ice Cube or dead prez record. My mind is much healthier after I switched up my media intake. I lost ten pounds of excess monotony and gained five healthy pounds of diversity.

40. The Message

ARTIST: GRANDMASTER FLASH AND THE FURIOUS FIVE
ALBUM: THE MESSAGE (1982)

BEFORE 1982 MOST hip-hop songs were feel-good joints. Joints that made you dance around dilapidated buildings. Joints that made you delight in good times.

When Ed "Duke Bootee" Fletcher, a Sugar Hill Records house-band member, wrote about the world around him—the broken glass covering the streets, urine-infested stairwells, roaches and rats as neighbors—and compared it to a jungle, hip-hoppers, including Grandmaster Flash, didn't know what to make of it. Not to mention that the accompanying beat for this seemingly depressing song was jive slow. Not a party groove. Not a "Good Times" joint. Melle Mel, who was convinced earlier than Flash about the song's potential, added lyrics and became the face of what would become one of the group's most successful songs. The finished product, "The Message," swiftly went gold, provided a framework for future MCs to lyrically delve into their environments, and proved that art with a social purpose (intentional or not) could also be commercially successful. We could rock to the thumping beat, be entertained by the relatable lyrics, and walk away with a message.

Because I was born in 1979, I don't know a world without hip-hop. Before I learned about the literary resistance of the Black Arts Movement, or should I say before I was self-taught through an independent graduate seminar, before I explored the storytelling of the Harlem Renaissance or read my first slave narrative, I knew hip-hop. I knew hip-hop as a platform for social change.

Protest art, or in simpler terms, art with a social purpose, doesn't have to be limited to a strict activist stance. It can be as simply complex as broadcasting one's reality. Haki Madhubuti, a forerunner in the Black Arts Movement, once wrote in his 1969 manifesto, *Don't Cry, Scream:* "The black artist by defining and legitimizing his own reality becomes a positive force in the black community." Rhyming can spark change. Grafitti can be political. Breaking can legitimize a young person's reality. DJing can facilitate unity. Hip-hop can serve important social purposes. And be dope at the same time.

I've never participated in a protest march. Nor have I organized a petition around a cause or initiated a letter-writing campaign. In my mind, the word "activist" is reserved for the folks who roll up their sleeves and solicit voter registrations, organize marches in Washington, DC, or lead investigations into inequalities. But, one day, a friend pointed out to me that through my writing, literacy initiatives, and teaching, I was engaging in my own form of community-building. I, like many hip-hoppers, didn't realize it, or want to claim it.

The idea of politics, activism, and social protest intimidates some of us. Often, we think these affairs are too far removed from what we do, or we don't want the responsibility of classifying ourselves as agents of change.

There's no denying that hip-hop needs hardcore, frontline activists. Soldiers and Souljahs. But we also need writers, artists, teachers, comedians, entertainers, b-boys, and businesspeople capable of legitimizing their reality and that of their communities. And, in turn, emerge as positive forces.

As "The Message" showed, we can package social issues with a head-nodding beat and memorable rhymes. Or we can lace important causes into a painting, a business decision, a hip-hop event, or a lesson plan. And in the process, embrace our role as agents of change. We can be aware, successful, and influential at the same time, doing whatever it is that we do best.

Send a message through your art, through your career, and through your life, and you, like Grandmaster Flash and the Furious Five, may be surprised by the reception.

41. *Be a Father to Your Child*

ARTIST: ED O.G. AND DA BULLDOGS
ALBUM: LIFE OF A KID IN THE GHETTO (1991)

THESE DAYS, GROWING up in a two-parent home is like being a member of an exclusive club that everyone else wishes they were in. Including me.

In 1990 a young Ed O.G. noticed a proliferation of nonmembers in his Boston neighborhood. "I always saw girls pushing carriages by themselves, but I would never see a family walking down the street," he told me. "At that time the thing was not to be a father but to disassociate yourself from any girl who said she was pregnant."

His response, "Be a Father to Your Child," is an early, direct plea to daddies to take care of their seeds. Placed alongside a mean saxophone melody, Ed O.G.'s calm call-to-action lyrics are so poignant that I wanted to rap them to my own father.

The absence of fathers in the home is one of the profound drivers of hip-hop music. Our generation benefited from the marches of Civil Righters, but we severely suffered from their walkouts. You hear the repercussions in the rage-filled voices of countless rappers. It's Jay-Z's mother stating on his autobiographical song, "December 4th," that she noticed a change in her son when his father left. It's the "Daddy syndrome," where daughters like me, Mary J. Blige, and countless others sought to fill the paternal void through self-destructive behavior.

My father didn't disassociate himself from my mother because she was pregnant. He became preoccupied with his own life to the point that my sister's and mine weren't a priority. So I spent too many years trying to understand and rationalize his choice not to take an active role in my life. I've feasted on a smorgasbord of feelings: hopelessness, resentment, abandonment, anger, and distrust. Fatherless children have a tendency to turn a truncated love into an intense, misguided hatred that we usually turn on ourselves. When we say, "Forget him," many times we really mean, "I wish he hadn't left."

But I refuse to believe that being a fatherless child is a hopeless situation. That would mean I would never be able to move past my father's decision. That would mean that countless women and men, boys and girls won't be able to either. At the end of the day, the father who walks out makes a choice that says more about him as a man than it will ever say about you or me as a person. So I had to stop using my fatherless reality as an excuse for victimizing myself. My father may not have always been around to see my potential, but that didn't mean I thought twice about reaching it.

These days, I'm learning about forgiveness. I'm working on developing an alternative relationship with my pops, who in the last few years has been making strides to have his presence known. It's weird to get to know him again. To do so, I have to accept the fact that he isn't a good father and may never be, but there are other roles he can play in my life.

More than a decade after "Be a Father to Your Child" was first released, Ed O.G. told me that to this day, people still come up to him to say that the song changed their outlook and made them do the right thing. It may be too late to play the song for my father, but it's not too late to create a new reality for this daughter. Shout-out to my pops. Better late than never.

42. White Lines (Don't Don't Do It)

ARTIST: GRANDMASTER AND MELLE MEL
ALBUM: GRANDMASTER AND MELLE MEL (1983) (ORIGINALLY RELEASED AS A 12")

THERE'S NO BETTER antidrug message than to see someone you love and respect strung out. Physically they're wasting away. Zombielike. Unidentifiable. Emotionally, they're empty. Mentally, they're one-tracked. Nothing else matters. Not even you.

Oftentimes popular culture celebrates and undermines chemical escapism. As in "cocaine is a hell of a drug," or the fashionable entries and exits into rehab made by Hollywooders on a daily basis. Some of us start to believe "I won't get caught up," "It won't happen to me," and more dangerously, "It won't ruin my life." These attitudes serve as the perfect catalysts for addiction to sneak up and capture the strongest, brightest, and least likely to succumb. Many of us who've had to deal directly with the ugly face of addiction know that there ain't nothing cute or stylish about it.

I was four years old when "White Lines" was released. With a trancelike bassline, the song is a rather subtle antidrug message that maintains addiction as "something like a phenomenon." For the longest time it didn't occur to me that the song was a blow to blow. To the casual listener it's your above-average funky party song, appropriate for any disco or house-music party. In the '80s "White Lines" could have been an ironic soundtrack to narcotic sessions.

An accompanying video, which wasn't officially released, is outrageous, an early directing attempt by Spike Lee that features a young Laurence Fishburne as the tacky yet effective drug pusher who services clients: pretty, ugly, young, and old. If you can get past the unsophisticated '80s feel, the video captures a certain allure of being chemically elevated.

In his memoir *Grand Central Winter*, Lee Stringer, a former addict, articulated that feeling like nothing I've heard before: "It is a taste I know I am going to love. The taste of success, love, orgasm, omnipotence, immortality, and winning the lottery all rolled into one. And then some."

It was only five years after "White Lines" was released that drugs would ultimately play a prominent role in my life. My mother sat my sister and me down to tell us that my father, the same man who was the big brother I never had, was a cocaine addict. It all made sense. His erratic behavior. His increased apathy. His habitual unemployment. The vacant look in his eyes. I shed one tear and began the process of denial and avoidance. Drug abuse remained an integral part of my family. I would go on to attend and avoid several funerals for relatives who lost the battle.

The pain and strain on addicts' family members is truly unprecedented. You're trapped between four walls of enabling your loved one, encouraging him or her to stop, washing your hands of the entire situation, and trying to discard the remnants that affect you.

Before I understood addiction, and trust, I'm still learning, I diminished it to a weakness that the strong could avoid. I remember watching a documentary about a young white kid from a well-to-do family who was diagnosed with dyslexia. His learning disability propelled him to drop out of school and to drink until he turned to crystal meth as his drug of choice. I thought to myself that he didn't have a sufficient reason to become an addict. As if he needed to endure some severe tragedy to turn to drugs.

But that's not how addiction works. I had to alter my thinking from judgment and anger to understanding. Addiction is an equal opportunist. Addiction is a futile coping mechanism.

That doesn't mean any of us have to succumb. Addiction is a dependence that can be fought and prevented. I couldn't tell you where America stands on the war on drugs, but each of us should know where we do.

"White Lines" may make you dance. "White Lines" might make you feel good. But as Melle Mel observed, the magnetism of drugs—the emotional euphoria, sensory numbness, vacation from reality, and the ephemeral erasure of life's problems—will all "blow away." It always does.

43. Children's Story

ARTIST: SLICK RICK
ALBUM: THE GREAT ADVENTURES OF SLICK RICK (1988)

I'M ALWAYS IN awe of the innocence of children. Anyone, regardless of color, age, or social class, is a potential playmate. At what point do things change? At what point do children who pretend to be princesses and superheroes turn into criminals, troubled adults, or jaded individuals? Is there a moment of truth, or is the shedding of innocence a subtle process?

When British-born Slick Rick sang "Hey Young World" and told me that the world was mine, I believed him. I was eight or nine, knew all the lyrics to the playful and inspirational song, and heeded his warning not to be a "dumb dummy" or disrespect my "mummy." The counterbalance to "Hey Young World" is "Children's Story," Rick's stirring narrative about a seventeen-year-old who goes from being a naïve teenager to becoming a stick-up kid, taking a pregnant woman as hostage, and being shot by police officers. At what point do things change?

Adolescence is one of the more vulnerable periods of our lives. We're trying to find ourselves and fit into our bodies. We're still developing mentally although we're already dealing with adult problems. Meanwhile, the adults in our lives are also dealing with adult problems and are sometimes unable to provide us with the tremendous support that we need.

Some of us were forced to grow up too fast. Some of us face a Michael Jackson syndrome, because we never experienced a true childhood. Some of us are so traumatized by our younger years that we struggle in the everyday of our adult lives. As a result, we don't have time to recognize the potential within or experience the fullness of life.

As I listen to "Children's Story" now, I think about cousins I used to play in the street with, innocent with bright smiles, who are now incarcerated. At what point do things change? Jail should never be a child's destiny. Something's wrong when young men believe that a trip to prison is a prerequisite to manhood.

My aunts and uncles have said on multiple occasions that they "feel for my generation." These adults who remember Jim Crow say that young people have entirely different and sometimes bigger monsters to deal with. And now I think the same thing about the generation coming of age. I feel for them.

All is not hopeless. The bonus about youth is that there's still time to guide (not that all is lost when we reach adulthood). There's still time for the loud youngsters on the train. There's still time for the youngsters on the corner. Some of us, including this adult, have to knock ourselves off that high horse and answer their calls for attention. As one educator and hip-hopper once told me, we can have all the panels we want about the plight of our youth, but how many of us are on the front lines actually doing something? He shut me up.

We don't have to wait for a mass "save the children" movement. Reaching out to individual young people can make the difference of one less child who turns into a stick-up kid.

I wonder how many children's stories would be different if they knew someone cared. I'll stop wondering. I'll start helping.

44. Stop the Violence

ARTIST: BOOGIE DOWN PRODUCTIONS
ALBUM: BY ALL MEANS NECESSARY (1988)

As I **WRITE** this, a ten-year-old boy and two teenage girls have been shot in Baltimore in broad daylight while most people were eating lunch. Police believe the gunman was aiming at a twenty-year-old male in a dispute over a jacket.

As I write this, a twenty-three-year-old man has murdered thirty-two people and wounded many on the campus of Virginia Tech. Thirty-two innocent people are dead.

As I write this, the United States is embroiled in a war in Iraq that has yielded thousands of military and civilian casualties.

"Stop the Violence" is a plea to end the bloodshed in hip-hop. Coincidentally, the song's release followed the senseless murder of Boogie Down Productions' cofounder Scott La Rock in 1987. And nearly twenty years later we're still battling a familiar violent behavior that is poisoning our culture. Rappers are still getting shot. Black and brown people are still killing one another.

If you know KRS-One like I know KRS-One, he makes connections with the violence in hip-hop culture to larger societal and institutional ills. The story is always bigger. He calls out vacationing presidents, war, and inflation to illuminate the complex threads of violence in America.

"One, two, three," KRS-One sings on the track, which implies that ending the mindless shootouts in our communities is as fundamental as kindergarten lessons. Even kindergarteners can grasp video games where jacking someone gives you points. Even kindergarteners can distinguish between gang colors.

Violence is a vicious cycle with emotional, economic, and psychological tentacles. A behavior that can be learned. Even kindergarteners know how to hit.

Policy changes and other high-level initiatives are necessary, but while Congress deliberates, what can we do on the ground floor to affect our communities? Can we shift our attitudes toward violence? Alter how we slice and cook beef? Provide our children with options and peaceful examples? Can families use the chainsaws of our strengths to break the cyclical patterns of violence that hold us hostage? Can we promote education like we do the block?

Give me a flower and a guitar, and I'll sing that "love is in need." Violence is killing us softly. And loudly. The "us" being the world. KRS-One eloquently states "Hip-hop will surely decay" if the bloodshed doesn't cease. This means, we will decay. Are we ready to stand up and shout, "Stop the violence"?

45. Brothers Gonna Work It Out

ARTIST: PUBLIC ENEMY
ALBUM: FEAR OF A BLACK PLANET (1990)

IN 1990, PUBLIC Enemy's, "Brothers Gonna Work It Out" foreshadowed that in 1995 black men would be partying with their bad self in their potential for greatness. Is it coincidental that in the same year hundreds of thousands of brothers of all ages, social classes, and consciousnesses gathered in Washington, DC, to work it out at the Million Man March?

More than fifteen years after the group's clairvoyant and hopeful statement on the promise of black men, the National Urban League released *The State of Black America 2007: Portrait of the Black Male*, which is as alarming as a Public Enemy track. According to the publication:

> *African American men are more than twice as likely to be unemployed as white males and make only 75 percent as much a year. They're nearly seven times more likely to be incarcerated, and their average jail sentences are 10 months longer than those of white men. In addition, young black males between the ages of 15 and 34 years are nine times more likely to die of homicide than their white counterparts and nearly seven times as likely to suffer from AIDS.*

In an urgent tone, Marc Morial, president of the National Urban League, predicts that if the United States "does not take immediate steps to address the black male crisis, the nation risks losing its greatest untapped resource." We are in a do-or-die moment. If Public Enemy (PE) released their record today, it would be called "Brothers *Got* to Work It Out." Have we entered the Terrordome?

The National Urban League is calling for specific solutions— including early childhood education, all-male schools, second-chance programs for high school dropouts and ex-offenders, federally sponsored summer jobs programs, and a higher emphasis placed on the importance of education. All of these initiatives are very necessary.

But as PE made forcefully clear, brothers must "get involved," know that they got "what it takes," and understand that their internal will is the most powerful driver for change. Brother-to-brother, black men must stand up and fight the power.

As a black woman, I know the strength of my brothers. When PE created a song celebrating their promise, I not only sung along with conviction, but I also believed it. And I still do. But when it comes to igniting the desire within my brothers, I cannot do it for them. This is a frustrating epiphany, one that hits many of us when we realize that we can't always play the role of savior for our loved ones. The longing to change their situation and become the people who we know they can be must be sparked internally first.

Just because we can't force internal change within loved ones, doesn't mean we have to sit back silently. I can support my brothers. I can rally with them. I can assist in productive programs and contact politicians. I can love them. I can rub their backs when they tire. I can let them know they aren't alone. I can pray for them. I can celebrate their achievements. I can stand by their side while they handle their business. I can get myself together in the meantime.

I can have faith. Brothers are gonna work it out.

46. The Listening

ARTIST: LITTLE BROTHER
ALBUM: THE LISTENING (2003)

IT WAS OBVIOUS he wasn't listening to me. My dinner date was offering perfunctory head nods and empty "hmms," but his mind was clearly elsewhere. Was he contemplating when his steak was going to arrive, whether or not he was going to get a little somethin' from me at the end of the night, or was he replaying last night's basketball game in his head? I will never know. But after I discussed, somewhat at length, what I did for a living, and his follow-up question was, "So what do you write?" I knew that fool hadn't *really* heard one thing I said. Although I was incredibly annoyed, I wasn't really surprised. Contrary to what we like to think, listening isn't a passive activity. But it seems to be a dying practice.

Years back, I interviewed Talib Kweli a few days before his solo album *Quality* was released. He told me, "I am starting to realize more and more every day that people really don't listen to lyrics. And it is tough for me being a lyricist, since that is what I am good at. So I have to find other ways to get people to listen to my lyrics."

Several years later, Phonte, one-half (was one-third until 9th Wonder sadly left the group) of Little Brother (LB), echoed the same sentiments to me. "People really don't listen to lyrics anymore," he said matter-of-factly. "You have to have a strong hook or beat." In other words, you have to have user-friendly packaging for your words.

You can imagine how horrifying this phenomenon is to me, a lover of words, and a hip-hop fan. How can you fully appreciate a hip-hop song without listening, dissecting, repeating, and remembering the lyrics? Hip-hop tested my literacy.

So I feel those LB cats on "The Listening," their tongue-in-cheek acknowledgment that while they drop their heartfelt lyrics, audiences aren't paying attention. Instead, folks are probably thinking about secondary matters, such as the condition of their Timberland boots.

Tuning out isn't just a behavioral menace to dope MCs. On various levels in society, we aren't listening to one another. Politicians are ignoring communities. Wives are blocking out the words of their husbands. Students refuse to listen to teachers. Civil Righters aren't interested in the rhymed voices of hip-hoppers. The hip-hop generation isn't concerned with the fading discourse of past leaders.

We prefer to ignore rather than listen, because listening means we'll have to own up to the trash that we're ingesting. *Yes, he really did refer to your butt as a donkey.*

We prefer to ignore rather than listen, because listening takes work and who wants to put forth the effort? *I'm just trying to hit that—who cares what she has to say?*

We prefer to ignore rather than listen, because it's a nifty defense mechanism. If we didn't hear it, we don't have to do anything about it. *Yes, former First Lady Barbara Bush really did say that being stranded in the Superdome after Hurricane Katrina and being evacuated to Houston relief centers was "working very well" for thousands of New Orleans residents because they were "underprivileged anyway."*

How many failed relationships, negative circumstances, and misunderstandings can be attributed to one-way communication where one party is talking and the other is actively ignoring?

Sometimes I wonder if it's even worth the effort to exert my voice when it seems like I'm talking to myself—whether I'm sitting through a wack blind date, trying to convince a friend that he deserves better in a mate, or explaining to students why reading is important.

But as Phonte told me, he is conscious of the new terrain of non-listening hip-hop fans, but the fact won't stop LB from dropping thoughtful rhymes. Just because some seem disinterested, unfocused, or distracted shouldn't serve as a mandate to silence ourselves. We should be motivated to push harder for our voices to be heard with the understanding that some will never hear us. Despite this reality, we should know that we have something worthwhile to say. Something worth listening to. Ya heard?

47. Don't Believe the Hype

ARTIST: PUBLIC ENEMY
ALBUM: IT TAKES A NATION OF MILLIONS TO HOLD US BACK (1988)

I **REMEMBER THE** first day that I learned I had been living in a bubble. I was attending an international black women's conference about globalization. I was excited, idealistic, and just happy to be around powerful women who looked like me. I really didn't know what the conference organizers meant by "globalization." My only understanding of the practice was superficially provided by mass media, which in different ways praised America's prominent role. I was embarrassingly clueless about the worldwide repercussions before the symposium. In an attempt to counterbalance prominent pro-globalization arguments, women of African descent from around the world—from places such as Costa Rica, Mozambique, Lebanon, South Africa, and Zimbabwe—gathered to discuss the very real impact that the integration movement had on their home countries. And it wasn't all good.

I left the conference with a heavy feeling. It was an amazing five days, but it was also equally discomforting. I had thought myself to be a fairly conscious individual, but it was at this conference, beyond the complex discussion of globalization, that I realized how much I accepted media, opinions, and texts as truth. The reality scared me.

Public Enemy's "Don't Believe the Hype" sends you into a state of emergency through a startling track, Flavor Flav's famous shuddering, and Chuck D's commanding tone. Therapy for my bubble epiphany. As the song gets older and better with age, its charge becomes increasingly relevant. A quick review of the current state of American affairs reveals that skeptical explanations (hype) have been used to justify a multi-billion-dollar war, terrorism, and broken levees. Various news channels that we depend on are far from fair and have no intention to be balanced. Sloppy journalism takes the place of investigative reports. Mass media outlets have more slants and angles than a racecar video game. Information is smacked, flipped, and rubbed down like a Bell Biv DeVoe record.

It's surprising that we can breathe with all the propaganda that surrounds us. It would be helpful if we had our own personal media assassin like PE's Harry Allen to tell us "don't believe the hype" at any given moment, but since we aren't afforded that luxury, how can we stop the well-oiled hype machines from rolling over us?

The responsibility falls on us to reevaluate how we acquire our information. Do we rely solely on mass media? Or do we dig for facts like we dig in crates? Are we inquisitive about the good, the bad, and the ugly?

Here's just one example that hits close to home. Because hip-hop is an easy media target, there's a need for us to question how our culture is broadcasted globally. A recent CNN special programming segment titled "Hip-Hop: Art or Poison?" illustrates that we are dealing with extremes. We may have to usher in the balance. Media literacy was never on my high school class schedule, so I'm self-teaching.

The reality is that we, including this writer, have a lot of work ahead of us. As PE declared two years after "Don't Believe the Hype," the next logical step is to fight the power. It's one thing to discuss the problems in the world and society's depiction or ignorance of them, and it's another to effect change in our own ways. We don't like how hip-hop is portrayed in the media? What are we going to do about it? Yes, we've got a lot of work to do. Might want to put *It Takes a Nation of Millions to Hold Us Back* on repeat.

48. *Fight the Power*

ARTIST: PUBLIC ENEMY
ALBUM: FEAR OF A BLACK PLANET (1990)

WHEN **DESTINY'S CHILD** sang that they needed a "soldier," in their very popular song with the same title, I was baffled by their definition. The men they describe, gangsta-lean in Cadillacs, sport an equally shiny mouth grill, have mad street credibility, and are equally as good in bed. Oh, and as the song's hook reminds us, they're very hood.

These are the men they want fighting for them?

Prodigy of Mobb Deep was dead-on when he rhymed that "there's a war goin' on outside." Racism. Poverty. Illiteracy. AIDS. Prison-industrial complex. Healthcare crisis. How can we fight these ills if we define our male soldiers as dudes with clean cars?

I know some of you are thinking that I'm being all Angela Davis and that Destiny's Child was just making party music. Blame it on Public Enemy. They proved that entertainers could also be political. It's becoming real hard to keep the party going when more than fifteen years after PE released "Fight the Power" many of the group's messages still apply: brothers are still working it out, we can't always trust mass media, and police brutality still rages. We've fought like hell for our right to party on

BET and MTV; when will we, as PE once suggested, party for our right to fight?

I was about ten years old when "Fight the Power" was released. I would raise my little fist in the air to the song's boomin' system. I wasn't aware of the magnitude of forces I would have to resist, such as racism and economic disparities, but PE provided a dope primer and left a lasting impression.

Maybe social ills like illiteracy rage through our community and corporate interests have so easily co-opted rap music because we're too occupied with superficial matters like putting television screens in our backseats, spit-shining our chrome wheels, regularly testing our street credibility, or telling brothers on the block that the whip ain't clean enough. Who has time to fight the power when our cars require so much attention?

The powers working against hip-hoppers are realer than cemetery plots. There is a war raging in our community, and how many soldiers, male and female, do we have who are willing to stand for positive change? How many soldiers do we have who are willing to fight all the isms? How many soldiers are fighting on the front lines, in our schools, with our young people, in politics? We may need to reexamine where we put forth so much of our energy and identify the real threats that affect our families, communities, and culture.

I have to agree with Destiny's Child. I do need a soldier. Hip-hop needs soldiers. But this hot girl with conscious thoughts burns for a progressive warrior whose car may be dusty because he's busy making the world a little better for his children.

49. *Words of Wisdom*

ARTIST: 2PAC
FROM: 2PACALYPSE NOW (1991)

I **GREW UP** in the home of an educator who committed her life to teaching. I spent my childhood summers helping her stamp textbooks in a musty school basement. It's no coincidence that I love reading; being surrounded by books for years affected my subconscious. I've spent an embarrassing amount of money on education because I was raised to understand its power. I put myself through college, then a few years later put myself through graduate school. Both degrees have afforded me opportunities that I would not have even known about without those diplomas. I will preach the importance of education until my voice is hoarse, and then still I will whisper.

As a product of a culture in which the unaccredited School of Hard Knocks (SHK) is one of the more popular educational centers, I also believe in the wisdom of experience. Some of our brightest have never stepped foot in a university yet still have a wealth of knowledge to share.

2Pac was a smart brother. He once told journalist Allison Samuels that two of his favorite movies were, surprisingly, *Ordinary People* and *Terms of Endearment*, films that are miles away from being hood classics. He was versed in the works of Shakespeare and said that *Catcher in the Rye* and *To Kill a Mockingbird* were two texts that influenced him. He was a student of life who, on a good day, analyzed his worldly observations through art.

In "Words of Wisdom" he assumed the role of urban scholar and philosopher, challenging the irony and hypocrisy that plague America. In a revolutionary tone, he provided revolutionary solutions: teach our children that the sky's the limit, and conquer enemies through education. It's no surprise that he was an avid reader and made the point in "Words of Wisdom" that he represented another kind of N.I.G.G.A., one who is "Never Ignorant Getting Goals Accomplished."

But 2Pac was also a walking contradiction who didn't make good decisions. He relied too heavily on a manufactured image to tell him who he was. He reminded me of so many young soldiers, so many of our SHK graduates who possess a stunning intellect but haven't fully developed the tools to fight the world with their minds.

"Words of Wisdom" calls for a balance where we use education as a weapon and learn from our experiences to grow as a person. Alone, the School of Hard Knocks doesn't always provide the depth of knowledge needed to dispel ignorance and accomplish all of our goals as 2Pac insisted with his N.I.G.G.A. acronym.

Along those lines, some of us with traditional educations seem to toss learning aside the moment we cross the stage. As if those four years of partying, finding ourselves, and cramming for tests was preparation enough for the beast that is the real world. What about all the gaps?

Whether you represent for the SHK, an HBCU (historically black college or university), an Ivy League university, or a local school that you could afford like the one I attended, learning has to be viewed as a life-long process. We all have to self-teach and seek knowledge like our survival depends on it, because it does. We should fill in the holes in our intellect through a two-sided process. Heads: investigate those topics that were ignored or left out during our school days, from historical events to life skills like financial literacy. Tails: learn from our individual and collective experiences and mistakes, regardless of how many stages we have or haven't walked across. As Martin Luther King Jr. so eloquently stated, "Intelligence plus character—that is the goal of true education."

It's not surprising that 2Pac declared knowledge as the key to strengthening our communities. He was a smart brother.

50. Planet Rock

ARTIST: AFRIKA BAMBAATAA AND SOULSONIC FORCE
ALBUM: PLANET ROCK (1986)

THE WORLD NEEDS to throw one big house party where different races, religious groups, social classes, and folks from all walks of life gather in the name of revelry and good times. We leave behind our historical baggage, guns, bombs, and nuclear weapons. The global bash takes place in some massive area that is physically too small but that the world packs into anyway. What's a house party if you aren't cramped and breathing in the energy of the people around you? Music blasts from the sky, and DJs from around the world showcase their skills. Everybody is armpit-sweaty as we sing along with the songs in our respective languages. No one's too cool. The impetus and anthem for this global house party? "Planet Rock," of course.

Sounds crazy? Maybe. But the Universal Zulu Nation, the organization founded by hip-hop godfather and master of records Afrika Bambaataa, has been promoting the healing power of music for decades. Bambaataa, a musical fusionist who is also a people fusionist, captured the Zulu tenets of peace, unity, love, and fun in sonic form. "Planet Rock" is more than a mandatory entry on a hip-hop classics lists or an orgasmic masterpiece—it is a global declaration that we are one. The track is indescribable. It needs to be heard to be justly understood. Soulsonic Force rip some of the most memorable call-and-response party lines that prompt us to forget the craziness surrounding us, to "love life," and let the "music's magic" replace the harsh realities of the world. We release our cares through shaking and bumping.

Imagine if our planet rocked instead of ached. Despite our different perspectives, we all get down with the get down. The good times consume the bad. Global beefs are settled through breaking or DJing competitions. Sound crazy? Maybe. But so does nuclear power and wars that span decades. So does hating a person just because of their skin color or their accent. So does living life angry and sad instead of lovingly and happy.

Whether we like it or not, humans must coexist on Earth despite our differences. We should explore ways to live with one another harmoniously, whether it's on the same block, in the same community, or on the same planet. I can't think of a better way to unite than through the power of music. And dancing of course.

Hip-hoppers could lead the charge, 'cause we certainly know how to rock a party. We can invite a few of our closest billion friends and enemies and celebrate in the name of breathing. Life is too short to consider blowing one another up or letting another angry moment pass.

51. *Hip-Hop*

ARTIST: DEAD PREZ
ALBUM: LET'S GET FREE (2000)

IF YOU WERE to survey people to define hip-hop, you'd probably get as many different answers as there are aspiring rappers in the world. So far, the most prominent definitions I've heard include a musical genre; a lifestyle; a culture that includes the four defining elements of breaking, DJing, MCing, and graffiti; and a corporate slave. Hip-hop has also been hailed as a news source for black and brown people; a tool for political change; and a global social movement. If you ask KRS-One, he'd say that he's hip-hop.

With a bass-heavy track that taunts the listener and sets the stage for powerful lyrics, "Hip-Hop" could very well be the culture's national anthem, mainly because of the song's hook, where dagger-spitters dead prez yell, "It's bigger than hip-hop. . . ." In a concise statement the revolutionary gangstas bring together the limitations and potential of the culture into sharp perspective.

Hip-hop is too many things and not enough things at the same time. It's been lifted on a pedestal for being both a political movement and a tool for social change while simultaneously being charged with being

neither. The reason for this disconnect is both simple and scary: we are hip-hop.

Dead prez forcefully rhymed about the bigger picture: getting us together. Our communities are vibrantly suffering to a droning beat, and we're waiting for hip-hop to drive us out of desperation. We continue to be taunted by the fantastical worlds celebrated in music videos and on WACK-FM. Who is behind the wheel?

Hip-hop isn't dead. Its power is dormant because we're not harnessing it properly. A few of us have gotten rich off rhyming, while the majority of us are still trying to find our way. No, we are not harnessing it properly.

Our communities won't change until we change. Hip-hop won't change until we change. We can't wait on unborn leaders or hip-hop angels to swoop down, transport us out of our despair, fly to the radio stations, and wreck the DJs. Nor can we wait for rappers who may be blessed on the mic to challenge community issues and conquer them. The power to effect revolution can be found in you and me. Until we learn to unleash the power within, nothing will change. Not even the dial on the radio station.

Movements aren't empty. They are filled with people who are hungry for progression. Are we satisfied with the state of our communities where poverty, illiteracy, unemployment, and crime are the real stars because some of us can drink overpriced champagne and not worry about how to pay for it?

What we choose to do with this inner strength, this dynamic power, is at our discretion. It's easy to charge hip-hop with the task of changing our lives, because it relinquishes our personal responsibility. But it's individual women who decide they want to get paid from shaking what their momma gave them. It's individual men who decide they want to get paid for assuming a stereotypical persona. It's individuals who decide they want to use hip-hop as an educational tool or vehicle to increase voter registration.

To open his first solo album, 1999's *Black on Both Sides*, Mos Def says in "Fear Not of Man," "You know what's gonna happen with hip-hop? Whatever's happening with us." On the same album Mos Def also has a song titled "Hip Hop" in which the Brooklyn MC discusses all the things that the music can do, including cut you a check and give you a beat to nod to. But Mos is clear: hip-hop cannot save you.

"We are hip-hop" means this is about you and me. We don't give ourselves enough credit or enough responsibility. This is about hip-hop. This isn't about hip-hop. This is about you and me. Let's get healed.

*Love's
Gonna
Get'cha*

PART FOUR

52. All That I Got Is You

ARTIST: GHOSTFACE KILLAH, FEATURING MARY J. BLIGE AND POPA WU
ALBUM: IRONMAN (1996)

WHEN HIP-HOPPERS, especially artists or athletes, score a lucrative contract and are asked what's the first thing they are going to purchase, besides uttering off one or more of the usual suspects—rimmed-up car, face-sized medallions, or monstrous mansion—the next most common answer is a house for Momma. Ask me the same question after I start clocking the big dollars, and my first response will also be a retirement pad for the woman who raised me.

When Ghostface Killah released "All That I Got Is You," the soft spot that I already held for him melted. Ghost reminds me of that grimy, crass, talented, and comical cousin I just can't get enough of. And with my favorite rags-to-riches (not just financially—sistagirl has grown emotionally, too) diva, Mary J. Blige, on the hook, there was no way I couldn't feel this song. Exposing a vulnerable side, Ghostface recounts heartbreaking childhood memories of when his father left and his life changed. While his mother struggled to raise her children and mask her pain, his grandmother "held the family down." The tribute to the matriarchs in his life has the power to make the most thuggish thugs cry.

When I was a child, it was hard for me to understand the many sacrifices my mother made for me. At age nine, when she told me that we would have to move hundreds of miles away from West Orange, New Jersey, to Baltimore, Maryland, all I could think about was the horrifying turn my life was going to take. My young mind couldn't fathom the immense burden on her womanly shoulders.

The role of Momma in hip-hop culture isn't forthright, although she's single-handedly raised some of our greatest as well as a significant majority of our generation. I always smile when I think about the story behind LL Cool J's *Mama Said Knock You Out*—which coincidentally was the first CD I ever owned, courtesy of my own Momma. It was his grandmother who told him to lyrically punch out the competition and critics. Momma *is* hip-hop.

As I grow older and life's responsibilities are made real, I begin to better understand my mother's journey. I am in awe of her strength and perseverance. I strive to be just as resilient and determined. No one has had my back like her. She is my boxing coach in the fights of life. She's my creative muse, and her intentions are always good. She understands even if I don't. Sometimes I get all deep and retrospective and ponder questions like, *Where would I be if it weren't for my mother?* Scary.

I remember those weird teenage days when I used to be embarrassed to be seen with Moms. On a hot Saturday night at the mall, such an appearance would have been detrimental to my social status. Now I stroll arm in arm with her. I need Momma to know that I appreciate her.

And that's what "All That I Got Is You" is about, paying tribute to our mothers, fathers, grandparents, or whoever lent a hand in making us who we are today. It's vital that we stop in the midst of taking over the world, doing us, and making moves, to be gracious. On gray days, uttering the words "thank you," "I love you," and "I understand" can be rays of sunlight for our caretakers. No matter how hard, tough, or successful we become, we have to remember that we'd be nothing, nothing without them.

I can't afford to buy my mother that mansion yet, and it may be some time before that's even remotely possible. So in the meantime, I make sure she knows that she's my life; without her I wouldn't exist. That's deep.

53. I Need Love

ARTIST: LL COOL J
ALBUM: BIGGER AND DEFFER (1987)

I'**LL NEVER UNDERSTAND** why some people act like they're too hard to love. Like being in love isn't "hood" enough, or loving someone somehow chips away at your cool. All I know is that at the end of the day, no matter how hard you are or how high that wall is you've built around you, in the harsh lives we lead, love is what sustains us. It is, as Keith Murray would say, "the most beautifullest thing in this world."

The "I'm Bad" MC, LL Cool J, may have lost a little street credibility when he sat in his room, stared at the wall, and realized that he needed love. In a documentary about his life that aired on cable, the Queens rapper said he wrote the hip-hop ballad at a time when he was touring and, although groupies were plentiful, he felt alone. Ladies Love Cool James, lonely?

As hip-hoppers, we pride ourselves on being survivors with me-against-the-world attitudes. But it's the relationships and intimacy we share with others that truly fulfill us. There's nothing more fly than sharing your world with someone who's got you, mind, body, and soul.

Forget what you heard: money, power, and respect, combined, can't touch the power of love.

So why do we avoid love like it's dressed in blue and issuing warrants? And why do we sully, adulterate, and screw it up, blame it for failed relationships and charge the emotion with a life sentence: *I'll never love again. Love is for suckers.*

I've seen a few friends give up on love or smear its reputation by telling anyone who will listen that love is overrated. This perspective is usually the result of a relationship gone bad in middle school from which they've never recovered. As a result, the dating pool is filled with schools of men and women who are afraid to love.

I've experienced two major heartbreaks and a few tremors. I've spent a fair share of time staring at the wall, tears streaming down my face, yelling, "Why?" Followed by a dramatic, high-pitched, "Damn, damn, damn!" My inclination was to blame love and the dude, because it's the easiest, least painful course of action. When I realized my thinking was warped and jaded, I vowed to never give up on love. I may give dating a rest, may swear off fools, and may do me for a period of time, but if love comes my way, I won't fight it. I won't resist. I'll submit to its power and hope that the relationship part works.

On the B-side, we have to be cautious of what we're willing to do in the name of "love," which may actually be "loneliness," "obsession," or "unhappiness" in disguise. It's not worth losing ourselves to hold on to someone else.

LL had it right. We can all benefit from shedding some of our hard-core posturing or knocking down the Great Wall of Pain to allow ourselves to be more emotionally expressive. I'm sure we've all spent time staring at the wall and wishing for someone who understands us and unequivocally has our back. Real love. There's nothing soft about it.

54. Tainted

ARTIST: SLUM VILLAGE, FEATURING DWELE
ALBUM: TRINITY (PAST, PRESENT, AND FUTURE) (2002)

I WOULD BE one depressed chick if I measured my success in life by watching television. Twenty-year-olds swerve in hundred-thousand-dollar cars while I pimp the 2 train. But I can be down with them if I acknowledge that for these players it's always money over b$tches. Happiness means being posted up in the VIP section of a club while half-naked women compete for a glass (or shower) of champagne. The quest for love is a contest where several dysfunctional strangers fight over someone they don't know.

And here I was thinking that the type of love and happiness that Al Green sang about are two unadulterated friends who will still be around to skip down the marriage aisle with me as I celebrate a union where even if my man and I live in an apartment the size of a Gap dressing room, can't afford cable, and eat tuna fish sandwiches, we can still revel in the fact that we have each other.

Am I tripping?

Call it environmental, but popular culture has either influenced our views on matters of the heart, or our tainted perspectives have taken center stage during prime-time television.

With the help of the bright musician Dwele, Slum Village, a Detroit-based hip-hop group rap about a love that is always free. In "Tainted" they give me hope that maybe I'm not the only unrealistic, idealistic naiveté who still wants a love as pristine as the Galapagos Islands, before humans started to contaminate them.

Yet when I mention this type of affection and utter the words "real love" from the hook in "Tainted," wise women who've been through the storm, old playas who reminisce about the good old days, and young dudes who are replacing older ones consider me clueless. Young women tell me to stop fantasizing about a fairy tale.

I know women who are only interested in dating men with six-figure 401(k) retirement plans, heavy cars, and disposable income to cover high-maintenance requests.

I know men who only want to marry a woman who can cook, doesn't talk too much, and who looks like a model in public. When I ask about love, I get the Tina Turner reply, "What's love got to do with it?" When did everything become so tainted?

Here's another inconvenient truth: many of us don't know what real love is. We either haven't seen it in our own families, or a dysfunctional version of it took its place. The act of love is very much a learned behavior, even if the feeling behind it is innate.

Reality shows have stumbled clumsily into the reality of our lives. True love and happiness aren't even sound bytes in our conversations.

Rather, they are like ancient theories that only philosophers are interested in exploring.

Hopeless romantic. I'll take that charge. Maybe I am searching for a nonexistent degree of contentment where I am with someone who loves me despite my Pepto-Bismol obsession, hairy back, inquisitive nature, and affinity for daytime naps. Call me Sleeping Beauty. If I don't set a standard, I'll settle for anything.

If we lived in a pristine world, everyone's intentions to love us would be genuine. Gold diggers would be two-dimensional characters found only in novels. "Playas" would be the slang word for athletes. But these constructs exist as living beings. And despite their presence and that of so many other antilove proponents, I still believe that real love exists and can exist in our lives. How can you put a price tag on that?

55. *Passing Me By*

ARTIST: THE PHARCYDE
ALBUM: BIZARRE RIDE II THE PHARCYDE (1992)

AS A THIRTEEN-YEAR-OLD who wore purple stirrup pants, matching violet hi-top Reebok Freestyles, and had a bushy ponytail affixed to the side of my head, I had a find-out-if-he-likes-me-through-a-note-that-my-girl-passes crush. His name was Sam. A bigheaded boy who straddled "class clown" and "young pimp." The note was passed. Or maybe the secret was whispered. Either way, I liked him. He liked my girl. That's the day I learned that not everyone will dig me. Damn.

It's no coincidence that my favorite song during this traumatic adolescent experience was the infectious "Passing Me By," an opus about the pang of rejection. In my personal angst, I had recorded the lyrics in a red one-subject notebook and recited Bootie Brown's verse for my sister's friends in that nasal, high-pitched tone. "Passing Me By" was esoteric cool from a West Coast group that didn't publicize a gang affiliation.

The video, which I taped from some cable music program, was equally amusing as a visual articulation of my pain. The four Cali dudes hung upside down as women—and seemingly the world—walked right pass them. In a culture where most guys don't freely admit that every chick doesn't come with her legs spread, "Passing Me By" is a breath of real air, minus the smog of BS.

The sentiment has stayed with me. Over the years, it wasn't just Sam who lost out on all of this. There was Derrick, Tyrone, Mike, Carl, and a few others not worth mentioning. I've made a nice fool of myself trying to gain equal parts of attention, affection, and reaction. Picture me in the kitchen, sweating, frying chicken, trying to settle any indecision through the stomach of whatever dude I was trying to get with. I've played wifey without the ring and the-sister-in-your-corner without any association. I've written long love letters (and e-mails) like Fatlip, former member of the Pharcyde, rhymed about in his verse.

In the end, these acts of show-and-prove got me nowhere. Left me hanging. Upside down. The obvious hit: if they're not digging me the way that I deserve, there's probably a good reason, and it's best that I let them pass.

That's not to say that rejection doesn't still feel like a rusty shank stab to a sista's self-esteem and pride. *He doesn't want to get with me? Didn't my mother tell him that I'm perfect?*

Age coupled with experience is a beautiful thing. You learn about how factors like timing, a person's own issues and insecurities, and chemistry play hater roles in your romantic destiny.

If you're lucky, you can look back and feel that sense of relief that you never hooked up with So-and-So in the first place. You may even taste the sweet satisfaction of spotting an ex-crush in the supermarket. Shorty aged twenty years in only three, gained weight in the wrong places, and pushed a stroller that luckily didn't cart your screaming child. You scratch your head and try to recall why, again, did you want to be with So-and-So? The reasons escape you like a smooth criminal. And without saying hello, you break out like one.

Over the course of time there will be some incompatible folks who will bypass you like a drop-top in the fast lane. And that's cool—you wouldn't want them anyway. But the key is to keep moving, because if you don't, how will you ever reach your true destination? By letting Sam and friends pass, I proved to be a better woman.

56. Looking at the Front Door

ARTIST: MAIN SOURCE
ALBUM: BREAKING ATOMS (1991)

WOULDN'T IT BE great if there were a pocket-sized device that at a precise moment would automatically shut down bad relationships, friendships, and work debacles? When that moment occurs, a definitive signal, such as DMX's booming voice, growls, "Get the hell out." And you run like Carl Lewis out of the front door, never to turn back.

Modern technology has yet to invent this device, although I'm sure demand would be iPod-high. So in the meantime it remains up to us as individuals to pinpoint the moment of truth that dictates when it's time to be out.

For a good minute "Looking at the Front Door" was my joint. I thought Large Professor was cute in a weird, talented sort of way. But it was truly the rhythm that captivated me. The track was a smorgasbord of sounds: Jazz? Check. Soul? Check. Funk? Check. Years later, though, I can truly *feel* Large Pro's narrative about his dilemma to stay in a relationship with dead-end signs, a testament that mirrors a page out of the diary I should be keeping to chronicle my truth-is-stranger-than-fiction love life. Large Pro elucidated the emotional roller coaster that many of us happily stand in line for, only to unhappily ride: being taking for granted; so close to leaving, but not yet ready; and loving a person even though loving them ain't right. In the end, we're no better off than, in Large Pro's words, a "burnt piece of bacon," which, if it doesn't hit the trash can, is either forgotten about on the kitchen counter or eaten with contempt.

I spent an excruciatingly long three years—which was two and a half years too long—in a situation, far from a full-blown relationship, with an emotionally unavailable, verbally insulting liar who deep down inside I really didn't like. Explain that. To this day I still can't. I shiver counting all the time that I lost and all the hurt that I gained.

Some situations require an emergency break, because if you don't immediately halt, it may be too late. A good friend of mine was in a ten-year relationship with her high school sweetheart, five years too long. Notice a trend? She grew depressingly tired of his inconsistent employment and teenage drama. They were coexisting on two wavelengths, so they could never effectively communicate. When she finally told me she was leaving him, she planned a celebratory vacation for her newfound independence. Only to find out between margaritas and nausea that she was pregnant. She's now the mother of a beautiful son, albeit with a man she is now forced to speak to. A decision that was made one night too late.

Timing is a blessing and a curse. When it comes to played-out relationships, I've learned that a grand exit can't be made until we're ready. But the question is, *What are we waiting for?* How many subtle and blatant invites, also known as signs, do we need to receive before we graciously accept?

Moving on when roadblocks like emotions, loyalty, and fear are involved is as easy as moving a refrigerator. To pass time, a myriad of excuses are made: "We've been together since we were teenagers," "It's for the children," or "I won't find someone else." But if we possessed the strength to put up with all the horse manure in the first place, wouldn't that suggest that we have the power required to walk out the front door?

Trust this lesson is a work in progress for me. But I do make sure I know how far I am from the front door at all times if things don't feel right. I may even map the route I need to get out. I don't ever want to be that lost in love again.

57. *Let's Talk About Sex*

ARTIST: SALT-N-PEPA
ALBUM: BLACKS' MAGIC (1990)

IT'S A CLASSIC scene from the treasured flick *House Party*. Kid (Christopher Reid, from the old-school hip-hop group Kid-N-Play) sneaks into Sidney's (Tisha Campbell) room while her parents are out. An empty house is like foreplay to two horny teenagers. In the midst of heavy petting (a term my mother still uses) Sidney stops Kid and asks if he has any protection in his wallet. He pulls out a decrepit condom. Not ready to give up, Kid inquires about alternative forms of birth control, but they don't have any. Now comes the moment of truth. Should they forget about protection and satisfy the intense desires of two teenagers alone? Or do they postpone the sexual escapade for a time when they can be smart?

Sidney and Kid opt for postponement, although Kid's naturally frustrated and acknowledges that most guys his age wouldn't care about protection. Just like chopping up medicine into food, a public service announcement (PSA) that wasn't preachy or unrealistic was slipped into this movie with a hip-hop backdrop.

There wasn't much sex talk in my house. That was usually reserved for the gynecologist office, which I remember asking my mother to take me to. I vaguely remember a conversation with Momma about the consequences of "heavy petting," and another discussion about cutting the "peter" off any man who violated me.

So when my mother heard me singing out loud, "Let's talk about sex" while doing the wop, she shot me a quick, "What did you say?" Before risking a showdown, my preteen self explained that the song advocated for open dialogue, safe sex, and education. The message didn't get past me.

Salt-N-Pepa wasn't the only early hip-hop act to approach sex from another angle besides Holiday Inn invitations. Among other intents, there was Kool Moe Dee's "Go See the Doctor" and Boogie Down Productions's "Jimmy." But Salt, Pepa, and Spinderella, a paradigm for a rap group, released a song that demonstrated women taking an active stance on sexual matters. "Let's Talk About Sex" is a charge to destroy the taboo surrounding open communication that folks can sing and dance along to, courtesy of the Staple Singers sample of "I'll Take You There."

It wouldn't be long after the song's release that I would take sex education in middle school. It was a scared-straight class that was fairly unproductive in providing any realistic tools to broach or respond to the interactions of sex that lurked in my school's hallways. Vivid pictures of sores, infections, and discolored body parts coupled with a religious-like touting of abstinence in a school where we already had pregnant classmates didn't turn me off from sex; it turned me off from going to sex education class. Still, I retained Salt-N-Pepa's jingle-worthy chorus.

We live in a hypersex society, where in 2005, according to the Centers for Disease Control (CDC), more than one million people are living with HIV/AIDS in the United States, with an estimated forty thousand new cases annually. We live in a society where sixteen-year-olds are getting tested for HIV and young people are acquiring the disease at alarming rates. We live in a world where men and women are having babies with people they don't even like.

One thing is obvious, we ain't talking about sex.

Before any of us knock boots (yes, an old-school term, but still a favorite colloquialism of mine), we should precede it with a frank, open discussion. If you've ever been caught up like I've been caught up during that moment of truth, you know it's not always easy to stop the flow and interject a numbing conversation about past partners, STDs, and birth control. But it's much easier to have an initial discussion than to deal with the ghost of the moment of truth that can come back and haunt you as an unplanned pregnancy or disease. More often than not, we think too late: *If I would have just used protection, slowed down, or taken a cold shower.*

When life or death is put on the table or the bed, it doesn't matter if talking about sex is easy to do—it's *Very Necessary* (check out this Salt-N-Pepa album for "I've Got AIDS," a PSA follow-up to "Let's Talk About Sex"). As the courageous ladies have instructed us, we can "push it real good," but be safe and smart at the same time.

58. Just a Friend

ARTIST: BIZ MARKIE
ALBUM: THE BIZ NEVER SLEEPS (1989)

WHY IS IT that anytime you meet someone of the opposite sex, the first inclination is to hook up? Okay, maybe not always, but I estimate 98.6 percent of the time. Between booty calls and the label "friends with benefits," the traditional role of a friend has been stretched, twisted, and remixed to the point that when I tell a guy that I want to be friends, he has no idea what I'm talking about.

Biz Markie, the respected court jester of rap, attacked this rhetorical distinction in his classic and comedic song "Just a Friend." When I hear "we're just friends," a little trigger goes off in my head. I hear Biz Markie's off-key voice and see the video image in which he visits his girl at college only to catch her tongue-kissing her "friend." Didn't your heart just drop for Biz? Mine did.

There's nothing wrong with being friends +, but we have to be honest with ourselves, with one another, and especially with those we are officially dating. Call folks what they really are. If they are a lover or side piece, call them such. I've gotten in the habit of engaging in a deconstruction of semantics with potential partners to make sure we don't have to consult Webster's dictionary.

Once upon a time, I was seeing this guy who told me that the females in his life were only friends. So I was more than surprised when, one of his friends, let's call her Ms. Outtanowhere, showed up at his house one day like a deranged woman. As he argued with her outside, she demanded to know who he was with, spoke at length about their six-year romantic relationship, and asked him to return her blue sweatpants from his laundry bin. The first question I posed to him after he returned from his outdoor verbal brawl was, to paraphrase raspy-voiced, old-school soul man Bill Withers, "Who is she and what is she to you?" Friends, right? And I'm sure he told Ms. Outtanowhere that he and I were just friends, although, unfortunately, our dealings were very main course.

The traditional definition of a friend doesn't include hot sex on a platter. Don't get me wrong—if two adults are comfortable and in agreement about their nontraditional description, then it can be on like popcorn. But that understanding has to be established up front. With the lines of friendship so blurred, it often complicates the already-frayed connection between the sexes, and we end up hurting one another in the process.

Crazily enough, I have maybe two homeboys who I know wouldn't push the friend envelope into sexual territory if I had to spend the night at their house. The rest of them would definitely pull an FYI, as one friend did when I stayed at his place while visiting from out of town. He told me, "You know if you need some lovin', I'm down. Just want you to know that." I thanked him for the information. Of course, when morning came, I would have to accept the fact that he would revert back to "friend" faster than Superman into Clark Kent. And for the record, I would be able to notice the transformation much quicker than Lois Lane.

This leads to the ancient question that continues to baffle the mind: can men and women just be friends? On a sunny day, my answer is yes. But most of the time, it's really *hopefully*. Friendships form the foundation of our personal relationships. But so does honesty. If only Shorty would have told Biz the truth, he would have been saved the embarrassment. No one wants to be played like a sucker.

59. I Used to Love H.E.R.

ARTIST: COMMON (SENSE)
ALBUM: RESURRECTION (1994)

IT IS SAID that your first love is always the hardest to get over. Ain't that the truth? Mine went down like this: I was fifteen. He was eighteen. Me, sophomore. Him, senior. Same high school. Mutual friend introduced us. I hadn't noticed him before. Most beautiful smile I had ever seen. Six foot four. Chocolate. Exchanged numbers. First conversation, remember verbatim. First date, horribly perfect. I gave him a handshake. Several daily conversations passed. He asked me to be his girlfriend. I asked why? He was speechless. It was cute. I agreed. Five years. Best friends. No one knew me better. Grew apart? Too young? He found another. I was crushed. But not convinced. It wasn't over. Defended our union. Outsiders didn't understand. No longer the twinkle in his eye. I left Baltimore. He stayed. Grew in ways he didn't understand. I held on even though he moved on.

Common's groundbreaking "I Used to Love H.E.R." should be an inclusion in all hip-hop history texts. To fully illustrate the depth of his relationship with hip-hop, he personifies the culture as a woman he connects with on a deep-sea level. He learns from her. They grow into one. She grows faster and starts to change. Begins hanging with hardcore gangsters, drinks too much, and does too many drugs. The woman he loves morphs before his eyes. Yet, in the end, he's still willing to take her back, with the hope that she'll revert to the beautiful woman she once was.

For me, "I Used to Love H.E.R." resonates on several levels. I can understand Common's need to reassess his relationship with hip-hop. Most hardcore fans, including me, undergo this same process. And many of us are saddened by the wrong turn some of the music took—a right toward senselessness instead of continuing straight toward power.

On an emotional level Common's narrative implies that when you love someone, you may have to allow that person to go and be. If a love is destined, it will return. Letting go of a relationship or a bad habit, for that matter, can be a gut-wrenching activity, but more often than not, it is a necessary undertaking to grow, mature, and progress.

Momma had to tell me one day, very blatantly, probably the result of being tired of seeing her daughter hung up on a past relationship, "You need to move on." Her words attacked my heart. She was right. And so I did. Walking away required me to find peace in the new arrangement with my first love and to be content with his decision. I'll always have love for him and continue to respect what he taught me. That will never change. But I had to let him go and be.

Thankfully Common continues to do music, more than ten years after "I Used to Love H.E.R." was released. He seems to have found a comfortable place in his relationship with the culture that he loves so much. He's branched off into writing children's books and acting, but regardless if he's blessing the mic or not, he'll always be hip-hop, because it's in his heart. That will never change.

60. *Paper Thin*

ARTIST: MC LYTE
ALBUM: LYTE AS A ROCK (1988)

I WOULD LIKE to think I have a fairly sensitive BS reader. Like a truck backing up, it beeps in my head when I'm being fed blatant crap. I've heard so much junk over the years that I'm surprised my hearing hasn't gone bad.

"I can't hang out with you tonight, because I have to prepare for jury duty in the morning." Prepare for jury duty? Beep, beep, beep.

"I would have bought you a birthday gift, but I didn't have any time." This he tells me, days after the fact. Beep, beep, beep.

"I told you that I loved you because I thought I'd eventually feel that way." Huh? Beep, beep, beep.

Now the subtle kind of BS, the kind whose odor is masked by sugar-coated conversation is much harder for me to detect. I become lost in the smooth, velvety words. Words that keep me warm. Until, they turn into burlap and scratch my skin.

Over one of the craziest beats in hip-hop history, with samples courtesy of da man Al Green, one of hip-hop's first ladies exposes and dismisses suckers whose words are merely "chit-chatter." The lines go in one ear but don't stay long. In "Paper Thin" a very young MC Lyte is clear that she doesn't play dudes or dig for their gold. But because she's been hurt in the past, she's extremely cautious about whom she gives her heart to and what words, from the mouths of suitors, she takes seriously.

Dating is often compared to a game, but it's more like a mini war. Games are fun. Dating has much more at stake: pride, heartache, sanity. As Lyte implies, dating requires you to be strategic. Figure out the other person's intentions, and decode their plan before they try to sink you or plant a victory flag. The mission is to emerge from the struggle with as few battle scars as possible.

Perhaps that's a tad skeptical. But it doesn't stop me from wondering what would happen if men and women dropped the battlefront. What if we spoke from our hearts and came to the table with substance instead of paper-thin intentions? What if we realized it's in our best interests to be straightforward in our speech and honest in our actions? Word is bond, right?

I'm a lover, not a fighter. And I don't like scars—they leave unsightly marks.

61. Love Is Blind

ARTIST: EVE
ALBUM: RUFF RYDERS' FIRST LADY (1999)

SHAKESPEARE FIRST WROTE about the transcendent powers of love in his play *The Merchant of Venice*: "But love is blind and lovers cannot see / The pretty follies that themselves commit."

Follies. That's one way to describe the acts of foolishness that we find ourselves committing when our noses are wide-open like the Serengeti. I can look back and have a hearty laugh at my foolish behavior like buying a guy I was dating a gift certificate to a men's clothing store for his birthday, only for us to stop seeing each other before I had a chance to give him his present. When the saleslady said I couldn't return the gift, I'm sure the dumb-ass look on my face was priceless. Amusing.

Love doesn't always yield humorous stories. There was a time when I couldn't understand how a woman could allow a man who claimed to love her beat on her. *That would never be me*, my strong self would say. *He'd never get away with that*, my crazy self would think. I would round up the Black Hoodies—I mean, let karma handle any losses.

So how did I find myself in a relationship that on a good day was only mildly dysfunctional, but on a bad day was emotionally abusive? I would look in the mirror and not recognize the strong or crazy parts of myself. They were either hidden or had completely disappeared.

When Eve recorded "Love Is Blind," she voiced the silent screams of so many women who were internally and externally dying. As the friend of a domestic abuse victim, Eve asks the hard questions: What type of love punches you? What kind of love brings daily tears? What kind of love makes you wish your boyfriend would vanish? The hook answers her inquiries: the type of love that will "take over your mind." At the end of the song, her friend is murdered at the hands of her love(r).

Surely Eve and Shakespeare aren't talking about the same love.

Caught up. That's not strong enough to explain the twisted attraction I had to this man. No matter what he did to blatantly disrespect me, no matter what he said to consciously hurt me—I. Would. Not. Leave. He was my way of hurting myself without me having to inflict any of the pain. Part of me thought I deserved the harsh treatment. Part of me didn't realize that I was worthy of a safe love. I was outside of myself, watching a weak me paralyzed by negativity. It was the darkest period of my life, and even when I think about it now, it manages to cast a cloud on a perfectly sunny day. I risked an emotional collapse for remnants of affection.

I once read an article in the *New York Times* about the increased rate of HIV/AIDS cases among African American women. The news piece, however, was very much about how black women love. The editorial uncovered the fact that many females sacrifice their sanity, common sense, and well-being to claim love. After I got over my why-are-they-airing-our-dirty-laundry-in-the-freakin'-*Times* reaction, the article held some validity for me. I did it. I know women who did it. I know women who are doing it.

I realized that I couldn't leave my damaging situation until I was ready. The same could probably be said of so many who are cornered in hurtful relationships. Ready is a state that you have to emotionally, physically, and psychologically prepare to travel to. Hopefully before it's too late. It took me three years to reach it. And it is a beautiful place. I see clearly now.

62. I Ain't Mad at Cha

ARTIST: 2PAC, FEATURING DANNY BOY
ALBUM: ALL EYEZ ON ME (1996)

IT'S ALWAYS A trip to run into folks you grew up with and haven't heard from in years. You remember them as they were and have no idea who they've become. Guys who had more girls than Hugh Hefner are now married and playing family man. Girls who needed Jesus have found him and dedicated their lives to the church. The good girl discovered an affinity for stripper poles. Guys who treated school like it was a low-budget game show are now teaching youngsters about the importance of education.

In "I Ain't Mad at Cha" 2Pac reminisced about homies who have grown and changed over the years. One went from toting guns and smoking sherm to being a righteous Muslim. Although Pac tripped over his boy's spiritual metamorphosis, he still respected his friend's decision. The song fittingly contains a sample of "A Dream" by DeBarge. The aspirations that we have for our comrades don't always materialize the way we hope.

But we can't get mad. People change for the better and for the worse. We can't project the life plans we have for our friends onto them. Even if our intentions are genuine, true friends allow the people they love to grow into the people they are supposed to become.

I know I'm different from back in the day. Still silly. But more serious. Still smart-mouthed. Less feisty. Ditched the Tims, but still love my jeans. Still love hip-hop. But can now hear misogyny. With each birthday I become a little more and a little less of my previous self. Some of my friends can rock with the grown me and others can't.

It's hard. When people grow, the relationship dynamic also changes. Sometimes it deteriorates, other times it strengthens. And occasionally we have to manually cut off friendships that have turned unhealthy. It's hard to turn away from someone who's known you since you were sporting Russell sweat suits.

I'm in this weird period in my life when all my friends are growing up, for real. Getting married. Securing mortgages. Having children. Settling down. I'm at zero out of four. It's kind of scary to think that my life and those of my friends are moving in opposite directions. And this is the point where selfishness and jealousy threaten to crop up. We don't want our friendships to change, so we secretly wish for them to stay the same, no matter the cost. Or we're upset that our lives are drastically different, so we're envious of a friend's engagement or mad that a homeboy broke the sacred brotherhood of bachelors. But how can we become angry because our friends are growing? Isn't that what we're all supposed to do?

The fact that "I Ain't Mad at Cha" was released shortly after 2Pac's death sends an even stronger message. Life's too short to get mad at what we have no control over, including the decisions of our friends. Change, as 2Pac concluded at the beginning of the song, can be positive. Sometimes it makes more sense to embrace than to fight.

63. They Reminisce Over You (T.R.O.Y.)

ARTIST: PETE ROCK AND C. L. SMOOTH
ALBUM: MECCA AND THE SOUL BROTHER (1992)

I DON'T DEAL with death very well. Never have. As I child, I used avoidance to handle the passing of family members. I brushed their deaths aside and, in time, would simply forget. In the process, I became desensitized.

The desensitization is fading. I'm older. And I'm being haunted by the spirit of my Uncle Ishmael. Not in a spooky, *The Sixth Sense* sort of way. He just occupies my thoughts. I feel his spirit. I see his essence in young faces on the train. I wonder what he'd be doing if he were still alive. I feel like I'm living for him.

Uncle Ishmael was nineteen when his kidneys started to bother him and twenty-five when they completely shut down. My father tells me that his youngest brother was tired of being sick. When I was five or six, Uncle Ishmael came to New Jersey from Baltimore to visit us and say good-bye. I don't remember saying it back. Did I block that out, too?

"They Reminisce Over You" is dedicated to Trouble T-Roy (Troy Dixon), a friend of Pete Rock and C. L. Smooth and a former member of Heavy D. & The Boyz. It's a musical celebration of their friend's spirit. "T.R.O.Y." reminds me to never forget.

The song also reveals that I had been dealing with death wrongly. The forgetting and subconscious blocking I've done has reversed on me. Now I want to know my family members who left too early. I want to learn from them, hear the stories of their lives. I want to make them proud.

Likewise, I know the time I spend with loved ones who are here and full of breath is equally as significant. When Ishmael's older brother, my father, suffered another bout with Hodgkin's disease and survived, I was grateful for that rare second chance to reconnect with him.

We all have developed methods to (not) cope with death, and many of us have found our own ways to keep memories alive. It doesn't matter if we pour out liquor, rhyme about friends who have passed, hold candlelight vigils, or speak to the departed at night. All that matters is that we never forget.

My deceased relatives are popping up in my writing. Uncle Ishmael wants me to write his story. Gladly. I feel honored to keep his legacy alive.

Life Is What You Make It

PART FIVE

64. *My Philosophy*

ARTIST: BOOGIE DOWN PRODUCTIONS
ALBUM: BY ALL MEANS NECESSARY (1988)

HAVE YOU NOTICED that successful folks always seem to have distinct life philosophies that have directly affected their achievements? I always wonder if they define these credos before their success or discover them in retrospect. I've heard tons of these guiding principles, many of which are explored in this book, like "think big," "act like a winner," and "surround yourself with the best." If I were to narrow them down and consolidate all these tidbits of wisdom into one all-encompassing philosophy, what would it be?

KRS-One, who considers himself a teacher, has lots to say about everything. In "My Philosophy" he lays out a sprawling collection of his thoughts about the world, the rap game, his art, his competition, vegetarianism, and racial stereotypes. He uses words like "dramatical" and spits several hip-hop quotables that MCs still cite. Over the years, KRS-One has held various beliefs on various topics. But as I listen to Kris, a former homeless teenager turned hip-hop legend, whose partner, Scott La Rock, was killed not long before *By All Means Necessary* was released, I'm reminded of the one philosophy that can universally guide me: *Life Is What You Make It.*

I know, you thought I was going to hit you with some profound, undiscovered knowledge that you ain't heard. If you're like me, you've probably been told the statement more than you'd like to remember and brushed it off as some generic silver-lining chatter. However, during one of my many days on the Grind as I worked hard toward my dreams, I took some time to actually stop and think about the statement's implications. I was instantly empowered. A bolt of motivation knocked me upside the head.

Think about it. No, *really* think about it. *Life Is What You Make It.*

The short declaration comprises all the mantras that I've heard previously touted by the successful. It encompasses the underlying theme of this book. When you know this life is yours to lead, you can decide to think big versus small. You can decide to surround yourself with the best or roll with a clique of cool losers. You can decide to give up when a loved one passes, or you can shuffle forward and make your time on earth meaningful.

Life Is What You Make It. It's almost cocky to think that you can do whatever you desire. It's overwhelming to consider the possibilities. I can start that magazine I always wanted. I can write a few books. I can establish an organization dedicated to literacy. I can take over the world. Excuse me as I aim for the sky.

Life Is What You Make It. I like to repeat it to myself. Now is the hour. This is it. This life. How will you spend it?

65. *Go Ahead in the Rain*

ARTIST: A TRIBE CALLED QUEST
ALBUM: PEOPLE'S INSTINCTIVE TRAVELS AND THE PATHS OF RHYTHM (1990)

I HATE THE rain. Chances are, if water is falling from the sky, I'm not leaving the house. My hatred of rain isn't just because of what it's known to do to black women's hair—my mane is chemically free right now, so water is an ally. Being outside when it's wet is uncomfortable. Slippery. You have to maneuver puddles to avoid destroying your sexy shoes. Or you can't wear those hot shoes in the rain, so you opt for the ones that aren't nearly as nice. Then there's the umbrella fiasco. Either it's lost, or it does very little to protect you from the showers of water that are mixed with wind. My friends usually save their breath instead of asking me to hang out when the clouds are spitting.

While digging in the crates, I stumbled across A Tribe Called Quest's "Go Ahead in the Rain," which I've since adopted as new motivation to get over my ill feelings. Q-Tip, member of one of hip-hop's most celebrated groups, encourages us not to let "the storm of life" scare us and to not let "a little thing like water" stop us.

My detestable feelings about this weather condition have made me miss several great parties, outings, and opportunities to be social. All because of the freakin' rain. I tried to calculate how much valuable time I've missed. How many days have I've forfeited annually staying in the house instead of enjoying the world awaiting me outdoors? All the days of my life are not sunny—in fact, many are quite rainy. Shouldn't I still make the most of them anyway?

My attitude about rain may seem ridiculous, but I'm sure we've all got some menace that seems insignificant in the grand scheme of life, but holds us back from living fully. Maybe it's not a weather condition (although snow has never been a friend of mine, either) that keeps you inside, but perhaps for some reason, even on the brightest of days you avoid the great outdoors.

In my heyday there was one particular wet Friday night when I had to face my hatred. I mean it was that loud, bothersome type of rain. I was living in New Jersey, and my roommate/best friend and I heard about a dope house party taking place in Brooklyn, better known as BK. I wasn't too familiar with the borough at the time, so I would be driving in the dark, in the rain, in uncharted territory. Being lost in the rain was not a predicament that excited me. My roommate and I wavered on our decision. Do we go? Buzz around the party had soared in that past week. It was an event not to be missed. We developed several scenarios to try to motivate us. Maybe it's not raining in BK, even though it's coming down like large animals nearly an hour away in New Jersey. Maybe if we wait a little while, it'll stop. But the bigger question loomed, *what if the party is wack?*

After too many hours spent going back and forth, we said f-it. Jumped in my Neon, crossed our fingers, and trekked to the party of all parties. It wasn't raining in Brooklyn.

That's the night I learned how they do it in BK: right. The duplex apartment was packed with beautiful people and even more beautiful men who shared similar ideas about how to party. The borough's eclectic vibe saturated the small space. The right music blared at the right time, conjuring up the spirits of Stevie Wonder and Biggie Smalls. I was introduced to a new world. I could have missed it all, sitting at home, dry, in my pajamas watching *Friends* reruns.

I'll admit it. A little rain ain't never hurt nobody.

66. Git Up, Git Out

ARTIST: OUTKAST, FEATURING GOODIE MOB
ALBUM: SOUTHERNPLAYALISTICADILLACMUZIK (1994)

I **DIDN'T GET** my first job until I was a senior in high school. I was a cashier at a local Jewish deli. I became employed so that I could afford to buy my boyfriend a stereo for Christmas. It was a small token for everything he did for me. Shortly after the holiday, I quit. Food service wasn't for me. Neither was working, apparently. I didn't like spending twenty-five hours a week at a place where I didn't want to be, only to walk away with pitiful, tax-depleted checks. I didn't look for another job. Why? My boyfriend took care of me. Allowance. Hair salon payments. Dinners. It didn't help, either, being the baby of my family. I suffered from what my friend and I have coined "YCS" (youngest child syndrome). As the last born, you're so used to your family doing things for you—cooking, purchasing necessities, managing household affairs—that you expect that sort of treatment as you go through life. Between my mother, my sister, and my boyfriend the benefactor, there was no real reason for me to do for self.

Then my boyfriend and I broke up during my second year in college. Damn, damn, damn! I was like a fish thrown out of an expensive tank. My lifestyle immediately downgraded. Financially. Emotionally.

Physically—I had to learn how to shovel my car out of snow. Reality hit me like Mike Tyson. I was one dependent chick, clueless about how to make it on my own.

Likewise, you may have stumbled across this character: the grown man living in his Momma's basement. He doesn't see anything wrong with his underground palace, especially since it's twice the size of his old bedroom upstairs. Living with Momma is rent-free, responsibility-free, unless you count cutting the grass and taking out the trash. Momma still does his laundry with hers and cooks the meals. And as she gets older, she doesn't trip about females like she used to, and in her bedroom, she can't smell the weed smoke coming from the basement. Life is good.

It's this archetype that OutKast and Goodie Mob put on blast in "Git Up, Git Out"—a boy, who doesn't want to fulfill the requirements of manhood, living at his auntie's house, sleeping until *The Oprah Winfrey Show* comes on, and letting life drift past him. The song's underlying theme? Independence and responsibility.

Hip-hoppers like to say we're grown, but how many of us are truly handling our business as grown folks should, where we throw the excuses aside, get out of the house, establish a career, and work to own a piece of America? There's nothing wrong with staying at auntie's house if it's a temporary fix to get you back on track. AOL keyword: temporary. As adults, we should two-step toward self-sufficiency.

Now I guess I'm the opposite of my previous self. I sacrificed many things: three-hundred-dollar shoes, expensive meals, and multiple drinks at the club (I've gotten to the point where I get one drink and hope that it suffices for the entire night. As I've aged, getting a dude to buy you a drink is sometimes not worth the effort), so that I could take care of myself. Forfeiting material goods in exchange for independence and a secure future is a worthwhile, albeit difficult, sacrifice. It's powerful to know that I can handle my business on my lonesome and that I got up, got out, and did something with my life.

This isn't to suggest that we shouldn't ask for help when we need it. I spent the majority of my early twenties pulling myself up to stand on my own two that I sometimes forget how to engage in healthy dependency. These days, I've been accused of being too independent. If I need something, like rent, I get it. If I need something done, like install my air conditioner in the window, I do it. Asking for favors is a last resort that I should visit more often. So I'm searching for a comfortable balance between independence and dependence. I need my family. I need my friends. And to the dismay of my feminist sisters, I need a man. But not to pay for dinner.

67. The Breaks

ARTIST: KURTIS BLOW
ALBUM: KURTIS BLOW (1980)

I'VE OVERSLEPT. NOW I'm rushing. Discombobulated and cranky. Skip breakfast. Get outside. Raining. No umbrella. Reach the subway stop. Soaked. Almost slip leaping down the steps to the platform. Train isn't running. Technical difficulties. The silver-lining folks would say that an attitude shift would make me see the sun. But these aren't those types of days.

Supreme rapper Kurtis Blow rhymed about the when-it-rains-it-pours occasions in "The Breaks." In his version your woman leaves, the IRS is knocking down your door, you've lost your job, your phone bill has hit the roof, and the mob is after you. Life really can't get worse.

In hip-hop the break is a defining element. In the '70s Kool Herc, a godfather to the culture, noticed that when he was DJing parties, the dancers went crazy on the floor when the raw instrumental took center stage and everything else faded out. To keep this short interlude going, Herc began looping breaks together to create an extended play for the dancers to do their thing. It became their vacation. B-boys and b-girls released the tension mounting from their urban environment by rocking during the break.

Blow, a former b-boy, crafted his song to feature several of these interludes. He stops rapping about the struggles of life and lets dancers take their frustrations out on the dance floor. He gives us time to forget about the world and lose ourselves in expression.

The breaks of life are inevitable, but it's how we handle them that dictates how we'll survive them. Think about the brown and black kids in New York who found creative ways, such as the four elements of hip-hop, to battle their broken-glass world and in the process sparked a global culture.

As the song of life continues to spin, a break will eventually come when we can air our aggravations, release our creative juices, and prepare ourselves for the next challenge. We must press on. Until the break.

68. Regrets

ARTIST: JAY-Z

ALBUM: REASONABLE DOUBT (1996)

IF YOU HAD the opportunity to go back in time and undo one mistake, what would you choose? I posed this question to a male friend who had a history of lovin' 'em and leavin' 'em. His response? "Nothing." He wouldn't change anything. When I shot him the Negro-please look, he explained that while he was sorry for some of the things he's done, he's learned to live with his regrets.

My friend could be full of the brown mushy stuff. But the skill of accepting our past is one that we have to embrace to keep on keepin' on. This is why one of my favorite Jay-Z songs is the underappreciated "Regrets." Not just because once the beat drops, it instantly speaks to you, or because the track features a mean guitar riff, but also because Jigga transforms a hood narrative from the life and times of Shawn Carter into a universal reality. The Marcy Projects frontrunner recounts his drug-dealing days when he maintained a third-person distance from customers to avoid the reality of his actions. He dwells on how his lifestyle weighs heavy in his mother's heart and wonders if any of it—the paranoia, the fear, and the guilt—is worth it. He strengthens the connection between choices and regrets by rhyming that his mother told him he could have the world, but instead he chose to push the block. You feel him. You look inside yourself. You think about your own mistakes.

Many of us are dealing with regrets just as heavy—addiction, abortions, bad relationship choices, and criminal activity—that we wish we could travel back and change. If they start selling time machines or magic wands that could wave away bad decisions, I would probably be one of the first in line, like folks do on Black Friday to get a half-priced television from Wal-Mart. Since the hands of time only move forward, we can only do so, too.

I beat myself up over mistakes, which prevents me from accepting them, advancing, and performing any reconciliation. I've witnessed people whose lives have been consumed by guilt because they weren't able to make amends for their actions, forgive themselves, and begin the process of moving on. I don't want to hold myself back.

To even recognize regrets, we have to embrace a certain level of honesty about the hows and whys behind our actions. We should perform the same introspection that Jay-Z's narrative does, and, hey, if it's easier to do it in a rhyme, go for it. While Jigga suggests that we should learn to live with regrets, I say that the only way to live with them is to first learn from them. I'm studying mine.

69. Street Struck

ARTIST: BIG L
ALBUM: LIFESTYLEZ OV DA POOR AND DANGEROUS (1995)

I ONCE SAW this proud-faced kid with a hard bop, all of about sixteen, wearing a shirt that read, "Thank God 4 Da Block." The irony of the statement hit me like the stench of leftover garbage frying in the Harlem sun. How many soldiers, mothers, fathers, and downright talented folks have we lost to the infamous block? It's like thanking Death for rescuing you from Life.

In 1995 Big L, an incredible wordsmith with a Nas-like potential, compared our fascination with the streets to the addictiveness of crack. Through an eerie backdrop of horns, in "Street Struck" the Harlem native tried to kick the truth to young block representers, many of whom we know: cats who pursue drug dealing like it's a career, folks who waste away days standing on the corner "actin' stupid, gettin' lifted," and the countless number of people who trade in real dreams for guns or prison sentences.

If we can't learn from L's provocative message, maybe we can learn from his tragedy. The day after Valentine's Day in 1999, he was shot several times, not far from his home and only footsteps away from my former residence. It's been speculated that the murder was a mistaken identity and that the shooter intended the gunfire for Big L's brother, who was also consequently killed. Big L had big plans for his rap career, but a block representer terminated that possibility.

In 2003, during the fifth annual B.I.G. Night Out, a charity event sponsored by Volleta Wallace (mother of the Notorious B.I.G.) where mothers of deceased hip-hop artists were honored, I had the chance to talk with Gilda Terry, Big L's mother. She described her son as a silly person with warmth and innocence. She told me it was a special night to represent her son's legacy since he couldn't be there. Two of her sons were murdered. How much realer can you get? Ms. Terry is not thanking the block.

So when I saw Dirty South rapper Ludacris in his "Georgia" video rocking a tee with the same slogan of reverence, I cringed. Why couldn't it say something more encouraging, especially with Luda's success, like "Thank God for Gettin' Me Off da Block"?

Too many of us believe that our destinies don't extend past the corner, a mind-set that shoots caps in our potential. There are other ways to get off the streets besides dealin' crack or shootin' jumpers, as the Notorious B.I.G. once declared, but it can't be accomplished by hugging the block like it's kin. While the streets may be able to teach us how to maneuver, the block should also be charged with being an agent of jail, death, and our destruction. We should celebrate conquering the streets, not the fact that the streets continue to overpower so many of us.

If we kick it like Janet Jackson and ask the streets what they've done for us lately, I'll bet the reply is a wink and a smile, while proud-faced kids continue to die.

I used to live on 139th and Lenox Avenue, the area in Harlem that Big L termed the "Danger Zone." And I resided in the complex where he was killed. To this day, as I walk the streets past block huggers and around hidden potential, I hope Big L didn't rhyme or die in vain.

70. Where I'm From

ARTIST: JAY-Z
FROM: IN MY LIFETIME, VOL. 1 (1997)

"WHAT DO YOU think about *The Wire?*"

That's the first question fired my way when I tell people that I'm from Baldamore in my hometown accent. That is, if I don't get the look of pity that is usually followed by "I'm sorry to hear that."

Don't shoot me. I actually don't watch the show. Not because it's a raw and perhaps honest homage to the drug infestation of Charm City, but because I don't have HBO. Even if I'm honest about my ignorance of "the best show on TV," folks are thirsty to know if Bulletmore is really as criminally minded as it's portrayed on television.

Yes and no.

Here's the "no" side. The relationship between home and hip-hop is a bond that is hard to break. It's from hip-hop that I learned to be proud of where I'm from despite my hometown's national reputation. B-More raised my mother and my father, my cousins, and my aunts and uncles. I was born in Baltimore and spent my formative years living, growing, and developing in the city's surrounding areas. It is a chunky slice of who I am. And it motivated me to be who I am today.

Superficially speaking, I learned many things from Baltimore: Don't hang around the parking lot after the club. Folks really do pop trunks and grab tools to settle beefs. Don't stand around a fight waiting to be stabbed—it really does happen. Getting your hair done weekly is crucial to your womanhood. And there's nothing wrong with a little neon green or orange in one's wardrobe.

I spent many Sundays cruising Druid Hill Park trying to get guys' phone numbers. My cousin and I would then head over to Eutaw Street for a chicken box and a half-and-half—a tooth-decaying, sugary mix of iced tea and lemonade. I love Old Bay seasoning, use it in my fried chicken, and do eat the yellow "mustard" in steamed crabs. If you throw on club music, our homegrown genre, I will turn into another woman. The music's bass will make me convulse. Don't be frightened. I'm just dancing, B-more-style.

Here's the "yes" part. Charm City has swallowed too many of my family members whole. Its daily news coverage always seems to include a murder. In this way Baltimore is like many places across the country, but because it's where I'm from, death hits home like Barry Bonds.

Jay-Z's "Where I'm From" is an extended shout-out to his Brooklyn. Over a nasty beat that makes you squint your eyes while bobbing your head, Jay brought his borough front and center, reppin' BK to the fullest, putting his hood on the map, and illuminating vivid details of a place where "ain't nothin' nice."

Jay doesn't reside in Marcy Projects anymore. I left Baltimore in 2001. I had to leave to live. To dream. In Baltimore I stopped growing. I stopped caring. I wanted more, like African Americans who left the rural south for northern jobs in the 1800s.

Many times we have to leave our hometowns to achieve our dreams. We have to leave to go to school. We have to leave for better opportunities. And very often the world wants us to forget about "back home."

If there is anything that hip-hop has shown, it's that where we're from will always be a part of us, whether you visit your block monthly or you haven't been home to your West Indian island in five years. You can keep it alive by representing lovely.

Representing, however, isn't just throwing your hands in the air and waving them like you just don't care when the club DJ shout-outs your city. Nor does it require you to go to great lengths to prove that your hood is still in you. It's unnecessary and silly to prove one's Caribbeanness, innercityness, or suburbanness.

Representing lovely is being in a position to help those "back home." I'm writing to get to that place. And maybe one day I'll create a "Where I'm From" in book form for Baltimore. *The Wire* is only a small part of my birthplace's story.

71. Love Vs. Hate

ARTISTS: BRAND NUBIAN
ALBUM: FOUNDATION (1998)

ALTHOUGH WE'VE YET to recognize it officially, hatin' is an American pastime. A reality that isn't surprising when groups like the KKK sprung up in the early years of our country's development.

As implied above, there are varying degrees of hate that circulate in society. There's that subtle hate where we harshly criticize anyone who is different from us, becomes successful, or we just don't like. I'm guilty of it. I find myself hatin' on certain celebrities when flipping through those gossip magazines. It's easy to trash someone you don't know, who's (not) doing better than you, a person whose feelings you're not connected to. And oh, Lawd, the Internet has escalated hatin' to a new level. Anonymity arms us with the confidence to type away, bring others down, and hate 24/7 without facing any real heat.

What I have a hard time understanding and explaining is an even stronger breed of hate that's taken on a dysfunctional life in the hip-hop community. Hatin' has always been a part of our culture (think South Bronx versus Queens), but in recent times it seems to have intensified and its popularity has soared, making it as fashionable as wife beaters.

In "Love Vs. Hate" those Brand Nubians call for the community to "eliminate that hate," which they believe is fueled by black-on-black crime, a lack of respect for one another, and a deficiency of love. Aren't we tired of hatin' so much?

It's clear that many of us are projecting these intolerable feelings on the wrong targets. Let's hate on the prison-industrial complex, police brutality, and poverty. Let's hate on those who slander education and those who celebrate their crack sales. Let's hate on rappers who hate on one another and escalate beefs into violence.

Conversely, as Brand Nubian acknowledges, there's a need to redirect our love. Onto one another. Away from the chase of money. Onto our children. Away from the block. Onto the pursuit of knowledge. Away from ignorance.

We should reevaluate how we treat one another. Extreme hate is not only bad for hip-hop, it is also unhealthy to consume and store the emotion like it's a body nutrient. It will only stunt our growth and we eventually become the victims of our own negative feelings.

Imagine if all of that collective energy that we use to hate on one another was unified into a potent, positive force. We'd be able to shutdown Bill O'Reilly (and others like him) and his hatin' on hip-hop crusade.

72. Umi Says

ARTIST: MOS DEF
ALBUM: BLACK ON BOTH SIDES (1999)

DURING A GRADUATE class that spent the majority of the semester exploring race, although it was supposed to be a literature course, I told about ten white classmates that being black can be exhausting. Our chairs were arranged in a circle, so I, the lone person of color in the group, saw the mixture of looks that registered: confusion, pity, annoyance. But none of the puzzled faces conveyed understanding. I was really too tired to explain myself further, and I'm sure they left thinking I was crazy or in the midst of an identity crisis.

Although that's what I said, that's not exactly what I meant. I would never be anything else but a kinky-haired descendant of African slaves. Just writing that gives me a bolt of energy and sends an electrical current down my spine. And simultaneously makes me sound silly for complaining about being weary when I've never been close to cotton-pickin' tired.

"Umi Says" is a heart's cry in which multifaceted artist Mos Def sings over a soulful track about his desire for freedom for his people. During the fight, he gets discouraged trying to do the best that he can with the tools he's been blessed with. Sometimes he doesn't want to be a soldier. Sometimes he just wants to be a man. I feel him.

I tire of representin'. I tire of explaining and justifying the minimal progress made by black people since the end of the Civil Rights movement. I tire of seeing my people dying and killing one another as their own self-hatred is illuminated and made powerful. I tire of the abuse of white privilege. I tire of the thorny complications when race meets class. I tire of proving that I am worthy and qualified. I tire of racism and ignorance to the point that sometimes I don't fight it when I see it. Disillusionment gets the best of me.

"Umi Says" is inspired by Mos Def's mother, Sheron "Umi" Smith, the woman who told her son to fight and shine his light. The tribute reminds me of how my own mother, from the moment I could breathe, instilled in me that I was a star, part of the solution, special, unique. Powerful. When I get weary and the pressure to unleash my power weighs heavy on my shoulders, I have no choice but to excel. I'm a role model, an example, a leader, and embodiment of the potential that my ancestors fought for.

One day over herbal tea, Sheron and I chatted like womenfolk do about hip-hop, relationships, and world transformation. She posed a question that I continue to use as motivational fiber: "How can we spark a revolution if we haven't had a revolution in ourselves?"

During those graduate school days in Boston, where I was one of few African Americans in my writing program, I used to call my mother to complain. Only to realize that I was talking to a woman who helped to integrate her high school in the early '60s. I'm sure she got tired. I'm sure she grew weary of raising two black girls. I'm sure Sojourner Truth got tired. I'm sure bell hooks gets tired. I'm sure Nelson Mandela is exhausted.

I find relief in "Umi Says." I'm not the only one who gets discouraged. Weariness means we're doing something right. If we stop fighting, stop doin' the damn thing, then lunch counter protests, hosed-down marches, and equality crusades were accomplished in vain.

When you're a chosen one—and I believe we all are, we just have to discover in what capacity—you accept the struggle as the plight of a fighter. You shine on. And we shine on.

73. Ghettos of the Mind

ARTIST: PETE ROCK AND C. L. SMOOTH
ALBUM: MECCA AND THE SOUL BROTHER (1992)

YOU HEAR ALL the time how powerful the mind is. My brain still cannot fathom its own strength. What does it say about us, though, that some of our minds resemble Fred Sanford's junkyard? A potential landfill crammed with thoughts that we hold on to, but should discard. Worthwhile souvenirs linger, but we forget they're there. The thoughts that we should use every day are stored out of reach, inaccessible.

In "Ghettos of the Mind" while Pete Rock is on the production boards, C. L. Smooth describes the inner workings of the hood—from crack vials to pimps—and how representations of these toxics grow like mold in our heads.

Often it isn't a physical ghetto that holds some of us back. It's the mentality that our environment creates that can be more dangerous than any rough neighborhood. In the ghetto of the mind, nothing green grows. Instead, elements like self-defeat and antisuccess hang out in the four corners of our psyche, drinking pints of laziness. Options are chased, booked, and held in a holding cell where we can't access them. "You ain't nothin'" blasts from our mind's speakers. Choice is left to rot.

Cora Daniels, an award-winning journalist, wrote *Ghettonation*, a book with the underlying thesis that ghetto is a state of mind. She points out that this mentality isn't dictated by how many trees grow in your neighborhood; rather, it is society's tendency to "aim low."

My father moved his family hundreds of miles away from Baltimore, Maryland, to the lily-white pastures of West Orange, New Jersey, for a once-in-a-lifetime job opportunity, but also, I would later learn, to escape the negativity in his hometown. West Orange was the last place he thought he would become a drug addict. Opportunity abounded and flowers grew. But not in his head. It didn't matter where he moved. He couldn't flee his environment without eradicating the destructive thoughts, ideas, and feelings that took his mind hostage.

It ain't where you from. It's how you think.

Many of us need a serious mind renovation similar to what's performed on those home makeover shows, where the entire house is gutted and a new one is built in its place. Afterward, we'll be unable to recognize the new home for our thinking.

Our minds should be the freest places on Earth, where our thoughts will be safe and nurtured. A place where we can dream and plan instead of damage and destroy. A place that's clean, where debris doesn't pile up. A place that invites information that will expand our minds, not contract it.

After planting mental seeds to help us breathe more fully, we may be encouraged to plant real flowers in our physical neighborhoods so that others can breathe easier, too.

74. Juice (Know the Ledge)

ARTIST: ERIC B. & RAKIM
ALBUM: JUICE: ORIGINAL MOTION PICTURE SOUNDTRACK (1992)

WHY DO WE classify ourselves as untouchable (check out notorious drug dealer Leroy "Nicky" Barnes's life story), believe that it won't happen to us (check out Eazy-E's life story), or wrongly presume that time is on our side (check out Tupac's life story)? It's as if we think we're starring in one of those blockbuster action movies where humans perform impossible feats and walk away unscratched. Some cats, not the feline kind, really do think they have nine lives and are willing to jump off the ledge to see if they'll land on their feet.

If I had the necessary clout, I would have nominated "Know the Ledge" as the first hip-hop record to win an Oscar for capturing the intense mood of the 1992 hip-hop classic *Juice*. With blaring horn alerts, the track represents Tupac's deranged character, Bishop. Rakim's narrative follows a pistol-toting shorty who meets his end in a symphony of gunshots. "Know the Ledge" is an expertly rhymed cautionary tale that asks if you recognize your limits.

In *Juice*, Q (Omar Epps) knows robbery isn't his style. He's a DJ, but instead of reinforcing his boundaries, he faces his own ledge and loses friends in the process. *Juice* is cherished hood cinema because it reenacts a concept from true-life stories of the hip-hop masses.

Many of us live with the expectation that we'll get a second chance if we mess up. Or more specifically, we act without considering consequences, and afterward we pray for a second chance. At least that's how I've done it. When I think about some of the nonsense I involved myself in as a teenager and young adult where I've stepped over the line, I was literally hanging over my personal ledge. Oh, but thank ya God that I made it through. And then I would try the deed a few more times. This sort of thinking is not just backward, it's also dangerous as hell.

Ironically, we constantly witness folks who have fallen from their actions. Yet we don't always translate their realities into lessons to learn from. As if in the end we're packing some sort of bulletproof, impenetrable parachute to save us. When does habitual drug use become an addiction? When does risky sex become life threatening? When does an abusive relationship become a death certificate? When does hanging with crazy mofos turn into a wrong-place-at-the-wrong-time scenario?

When we're knee-deep in a situation, our vision is dark and tunneled. The ledge is no longer in eyesight. Being cautious and establishing limits that act as bright yellow police tape to mark off our boundaries can save us from throbbing headaches, sleepless nights, unwanted consequences, and bargaining with God where we plead, "Please Lord if you get me out of this, I promise I'll never do it again."

I don't trust Luck with my livelihood. And if you're like me, a horrible gambler, it's best to know the ledge.

75. Mind Playing Tricks on Me

ARTIST: GETO BOYS
ALBUM: WE CAN'T BE STOPPED (1991)

I **'VE NEVER PURSUED** a life of crime, because quite frankly, I'm too damn paranoid. Shook. I don't have the heart for it. People are crazy, and revenge can be a helluva drug. I would rather not spend my days and nights frozen in fear, waiting for rivals or the po-lice to kick in my door. I already worry too much in my regular day-to-day.

As much as some rap music has glamorized a trife life, there are those gems to counterbalance the claim and show the dangerous sport of boxing with Death. On the realness radar, I give "Mind Playing Tricks on Me" a ten. I never hung up a poster of the Houston rap group, but this remains one of the dopest hip-hop songs, and it could have aired on television as an anticrime public service announcement. Over the backdrop of an Isaac Hayes sample, which provided an extra dose of soul, the Geto Boys are lyrically convincing that when you're doing dirt, it'll start to smell, and it's only a matter of time before someone comes to take out the garbage. The paranoia they describe doesn't sound pleasurable: Every several seconds you're checking out the window, fearful for your life. Bad deeds come back to haunt you. You try to pray for forgiveness. Regret weighs heavy on your heart. Fear is your companion but not your friend. You stare at the walls and they stare back. Nerves are shot. Your dreams are filled with adversaries taking you down. The only place free of worry is death.

Is it worth it?

Some movies and other fantastical creations would have us believe that we can get away scot-free from a trife life to chill on an island as our paranoia blows in the wind. When's the last time you heard someone retiring safely from dirt without first turning their life around? Prison or death. Prison or death.

These examples may seem far removed from the lives of Mr. or Ms. Average Joe, but when you're doing dirt—cheatin', lyin', sneakin', schemin', and stealin'—it's bound to catch up with you. Infidelity, extortion, blackmail, cover-ups, illegal hustles are all dirt with a different face. I know it's hard to believe in repercussions when folks from presidents to police officers get away with murder. But that's precisely the point. We can't base our actions on what we think someone else escaped.

Paranoia is rooted in the reality of our consequences. You can't run from it, no matter how tough you are. It threatens the fine threads of your sanity until that fateful day comes. And trust, that day—in one variation or another—will come.

I ain't saying that I should have wings attached to my back and a crown on my head, but I know my limitations. Staying up at night choked with paranoia is one of them. I need my sleep. So I try to avoid dark, dead-end alleys that lead to dirt. I need my mind to concentrate on more important matters.

76. *Check Yo Self*

ARTIST: ICE CUBE, FEATURING DAS EFX
ALBUM: THE PREDATOR (1992)

THERE ARE NUMEROUS moments in my life when I feel like body slamming someone. WWF-style, without a protective mat. The potential victims vary: the slow cashier with the attitude who works at the supermarket; a dude at the club who invades my space with vomit breath; and nondriving idiots who cut me off on the highway. Within a split second, I can visualize myself successfully crushing my victim and walking away, proudly and unscratched.

But that isn't how it would go down. More than likely I would catch a charge. A sista does not look good in prison garb. So I restrain myself by any means necessary—clench my fists and hold them behind my back, do that backward-counting thing my mother used to do, call on Jesus—or whatever it takes to defuse my anger.

I was in middle school when Ice Cube, who was still embroiled in gangsterism, released "Check Yo Self." Immediately those three words became a precursor to an argument or brawl among my classmates. Although I was never a fighting chick, I found myself using the phrase to cut back anyone who wanted to turn me into one. While Cube's somewhat dysfunctional advice was mainly for enemies on how to avoid shotgun bullets, there's no denying that our world would be a safer and saner place if folks, including our presidents, would check themselves.

If you're lucky you have people around you who let you know when you're tripping. It might be your boy who escorts you out of the club and saves you from a potential throw down and a jail visit. It might be your girl-friend who lets you know that sitting outside a dude's house isn't cool—it really is stalker behavior. Honest friends let you know when you need to fall back, slow down, or chill out. They put you in your place, and you appreci-ate them for it. Sometimes we need that rough, rugged, and raw love.

But we can't always rely on others to monitor our behavior. And this is when I hear Cube's ghetto psychology in my ear. We have to get in the habit of being able to put ourselves in place. It ain't easy. It necessitates an incredible awareness of who we are as individuals. It also requires know-ing how to rectify our behavior once we identify the problem.

Psychologists might call this self-reflection, and it takes a certain level of maturity. I'm sure Ice Cube had to check himself on many occa-sions over the years, because if he didn't, there would be no *Friday*, *Barbershop*, or grown-up Cube. Once you realize that the stakes are indeed high and that you have much more to risk than school suspension or parental punishment—like a career, family, and reputation—your per-spective on body slamming should change. It still perplexes me why mil-lionaire rappers run around like they're still hotheaded youth in the hood, catching charges, pleading no contest, and paying lawyers. It isn't about being the bigger person. It's about being the smarter one.

As I get older and I find myself succumbing to anger, I have to take a minute and ask myself, *Why did I just go off like that? That was stupid. I could have turned a minute situation into an ugly, drawn-out one, just by acting on an inflamed impulse.* Sometimes our raw reaction needs to be cut with a dose of reality. Now I know exactly why Momma counted backward.

77. Get By

ARTIST: TALIB KWELI
ALBUM: QUALITY (2002)

THE STREETS OF Harlem have a magnetic energy. Uptown stays busy from midnight to the break of dawn. Mothers pull reluctant children alongside them. Street vendors hawk everything you don't need. Old men talk smack on the corner. But below the surface, not just in Uptown, but in Yourcity, USA, more often than not, is an underlying sense of emptiness. Within the struggle to make ends meet, dreams and passions are smoldered. Wasted potential spills into the streets.

"Get By," one of Kweli's more commercially successful joints, is a wake-up call with soul. It sports a hook that makes you sing along like you're part of the choir. Kweli summarizes the song's purpose on the album's track notes, where he writes, "Every day folks wake up not to live, but to get by. This is why we accept our place in poverty, sorrow, misery, etc. Don't just try to get by that s***, Get Out! Like Bob Marley said, 'Wake up and live.'"

Some of us are living minimum wage–style, but not just in a financial sense. We are *existing* at a minimal level. Living life as if it were a day trip, packing just enough mental capacity and desire to get through the day.

Kweli raps that we sell crack, work until our backs break, smoke weed, and drink, just to get by. Hopelessness makes us turn to quick fixes for relief.

The behavior of maintaining instead of excelling is laced in our language and mentality as much as it's seen in our actions. I've caught myself on several occasions answering "makin' it" or "payin' the rent" as a response to how I'm doing. I even say it in a just-came-from-the-cotton-fields voice. We've got to be more. We've got to want more. We've got to expect more.

Maybe we wouldn't just get by if we believed we had somewhere to go. Toward a passion. Toward a purpose. Toward love. In this harsh world, it's necessary to search for and embrace a motive for living abundantly. When you know that your life is valuable, your perspective naturally changes from getting by to elevation.

The album that followed Kweli's *Quality*, which featured "Get By," was titled *Beautiful Struggle*. Beautiful. Struggle. The oxymoron, which Kweli said was coined by former groupmate Mos Def, powerfully and simply describes this crazy existence, this unpredictable journey called life. It explains why in one day a loved one can die and a child is born. It's not easy to balance the two opposites. I don't need data from a professional study to know that those who are happiest embrace life as a full-fledged journey, a roller-coaster ride where they play an active role.

Armed with the realization that life is both amazing and arduous, complacency should have no place in our lives. Our words, thoughts, and actions should soar. When we're close to the edge, we should fly.

78. *Take Me*

ARTIST: JEAN GRAE
ALBUM: THE BOOTLEG OF THE BOOTLEG EP (2003)

WE **WENT TO** middle and high school together. He was a clown. Had jokes for days. Told me I had a Jheri curl, even though I didn't. Cracked on me on several occasions. We argued about it. His clique and my crew would meet up at the mall together as annoying preteens. Was he troubled then? In high school we drifted apart, but he was always a character. He wrote in my senior yearbook that I was still cool even though I'd had a Jheri curl in middle school.

The way I heard it, much of it hearsay, he was found with his wrists slit and a knife in his chest. The door to his dorm room was blocked with furniture. A friend found him. Dead.

That was several years ago, and I still don't know what really happened. Some say he was having a tough time. Some say they don't believe it could have been suicide. To this day I don't *want* it to have been suicide. It's said that people end their lives when they lose hope, when pain outweighs their personal resources to deal with life's problems.

Jean Grae's "Take Me" begins with a remixed snippet of Psalm 23, "Yea though I walk through the valley . . . ," and then catapults into a painful prayer to God to either restore her strength or to speed up death. Depression has hit hard. Grae rhymes that she doesn't feel equipped to fulfill His master plan for her life. There's a knife on the floor and a gun in her hand. It's dark and depressing as hell. It's eerie and harsh. It is, for lack of a better word, *real*.

While there is a torrent of issues affecting the hip-hop generation, one that is incredibly prevailing, but rarely discussed, is mental health, despite the fact that many of our pathologies play out to a thumping beat over the television and radio airwaves. For another musical reference, check the Notorious B.I.G.'s "Suicidal Thoughts," one of the boldest and most unsettling displays of self-hatred, from his aptly titled *Ready to Die* album.

Like the generation before us, there's this belief that as hip-hoppers we are too strong to be "weak-minded." Or we're too busy with the daily struggle of existing to concern ourselves with psychological problems. Meanwhile, some of us who smile during the day are silently suffering, sitting alone at home with a knife on the floor. Pain that we've been hoarding for years eats up our insides. And in the early and late hour of depression and other mental illnesses, some of us can be found self-medicating, a tragically ineffective solution. But we're survivors, right?

We are incredibly tough but we have to recognize that even the strong need help. We should care for our minds the way we look after our cars: meticulously, lovingly, and often. With the world weighing heavily on our shoulders, we shouldn't be afraid to seek healthy coping mechanisms, including therapy and counseling, to maintain our mental power.

I still think about my friend. And I still don't know what really happened. But I do know that we need to take care of one another like soldiers in battle actually do. None of us should be left behind silently in pain.

79. Tearz

ARTIST: WU-TANG CLAN
ALBUM: ENTER THE WU-TANG: 36 CHAMBERS (1993)

IN THE PAST, if my father telephoned me, I didn't concern myself with calling him back. He had blown it as a father, and I was acting accordingly by blowing him off. Thwarting his efforts to form a relationship was quite empowering at the time.

Then he suddenly fell ill. The doctors didn't know what was wrong with him. Was it a return of Hodgkin's disease? Stroke? All the doctors could tell us was that his condition was serious. Serious? I was jolted into a fear that the anger frozen inside me wouldn't have an opportunity to melt. Instead I would spend the rest of my life fighting guilt and combating regret. I wasn't ready to talk to him regularly, but I wasn't ready for him to go, either. I prayed for a second chance with my father.

Within the warped lyrical framework of "Tearz" lies a warning about our frivolous dismissal of the fragility of life. One minute we're laughing, and in the next our lives could be hit with tragedy. The hook, provided by a coarse but fitting old-school sample, declares that after the laughter come the tears.

Some couples practice the rule that they won't go to bed angry with each other. I can testify that I've been mad at a mate overnight, through the weekend, and into spanning weeks. My perspective is changing now. Death is quicker than I am. One minute you're arguing with a loved one, and just hours later you receive news that he has fallen ill or passed away. The argument becomes trivial. You pray for his recovery. You pray for another chance. You pray for more laughter.

It's scary when I contemplate the uncertainty of our worlds and those of our loved ones. It's terrifying to think that in a split second the delicate balance of our everyday could be drastically changed forever. When you ponder life from this perspective, is that argument you had with your friend worth it? Knowing that one arbitrary day he or she may not be around on the receiving end?

This is similar to the thought process that I went through when my father became sick. I love him. I'm angry with him. Our time here is short. He's wasted much of it. I've wasted much of it. We don't have much left to waste.

God granted my request. My father is here. Alive. I think he's still here because we have unfinished business. These days when I'm tempted not to answer his call, I pick up the phone and we talk.

80. *We Will Survive*

ARTIST: NAS

ALBUM: I AM . . . (1999)

I REMEMBER THE day that Tupac was shot in Las Vegas. I was in high school and my boyfriend and I were startled, but we figured he'd pull through because that's what Tupac did. When he didn't, it was hard to comprehend, like the sudden death of a family member.

I can recall the day, like it happened last Sunday, when I heard that the Notorious B.I.G. had been murdered. I was heading back home from a day of shopping at the mall, car dancing to the radio when the announcement was made. Biggie was gone. Complete disbelief flushed over me. I rushed home, called the same boyfriend, and we both sat on the phone in disbelief. It was *unbelievable.*

I was living in New Jersey when news of Jam Master Jay's death reached me. I remember sitting in my kitchen, reading the online coverage and feeling numb. At the time, I was writing for various publications about music and cultural connections. I declared his murder hip-hop treason. How does someone kill Jam Master Jay?

In "We Will Survive" Nas performs his own reminiscing and retrospection. He speaks directly to Biggie after his death and talks openly to a deceased Tupac. He then ponders the rise-and-fall experiences of other black male entertainers from Al Green to the Commodores and spits one of the most profound lines that could express the state of hip-hop: "I thought I made it, but we only took baby steps."

We thought we made it, but in some regards the hip-hop generation has taken only baby steps in various aspects of our development. We've made leaps commercially, but mentally, emotionally, psychologically, sometimes it only seems like minor advancements. Hip-hop is known throughout the world, but some of us have taken only small strides toward securing our own survival.

Hip-hop has suffered many peaks and valleys in its relatively short life. Sometimes it feels like we experience more lows than highs. Is this because our lows are broadcasted and celebrated much more than our peaks? It's hard to heal when others pick at our scabs but don't offer constructive solutions for wellness. It's difficult to get better when we don't know how to begin the healing process.

But it is evident, many of us are tired of the violence, negativity, self-destruction, and complacency that the damaged parts of hip-hop perpetuate. Likewise, we're tired of seeing these elements play out in the communities where we live, work, and play. Many of us are ready to heal.

Even with all the blows that the hip-hop community has suffered, we have still survived despite our existence being questioned from the beginning. Our essence is a combination of old-school and new-school resistance. Granted, it doesn't always feel like we are a mighty structure when destructive tsunamis of corporate interests, greed, and ignorance blow through our community and our formation sways. We are built for adversity. A fact we should never forget.

It can be deemed ironic that Nas, the same artist who said "We Will Survive," also said, "Hip Hop Is Dead." I get it. We're in a valley. We will rise.

H-U-S-T-LE

PART SIX

81. *You Talk Too Much*

ARTIST: RUN-D.M.C.
ALBUM: KING OF ROCK (1985)

HOW MANY "RAPPERS" have you met who claim they are going to be the next Jay-Z, but when you ask them about a demo, studio time, or their plans to achieve this dream, they don't have anything to say? Or how many "entrepreneurs" do you know who have yet to write a word of a business plan or engage in any company-building activities?

I call it the "Big Thang Theory." And it doesn't just affect wannabe rappers. I've met countless "entrepreneurs," "visionaries," and "movers and shakers" who don't move or shake. They talk.

This is usually how a conversation with a Big Thang Theorist goes:

You: *"What's up?"*

BIG THANG THEORIST: *"You know, just doing big thangs."*

You: *"Really? Like what?"*

BIG THANG THEORIST: *"You know, big thangs."*

You: *"Like what?"*

BIG THANG THEORIST: *"You know, big thangs. I can't really get into all the details."*

YOU: *"Okay, but like what kind of things?"*

BIG THANG THEORIST: *"Damn, why you always asking me these questions? You're such a hater."*

A Big Thang Theorist's conversation is as empty as his or her actions. They've got big dreams and bigger moves that never materialize.

"You Talk Too Much" is a classic banger from the seminal Queens hip-hop group. Run and D.M.C. engage in the best of relay rhyming to put a "big-mouth clown" on blast who never stops yapping about his girl, the places he never goes, neighborhood gossip, and everything in between. He's a Big Thang Theorist, among other things. Run-D.M.C.'s advice for him? "Shut up."

Hip-hop was built upon a show-and-prove rock-steady ground. If you make a claim, you best back it up with hard evidence. So why do so many of us talk about what we're going to do without ever doing it?

There's a multitude of reasons, but the most popular culprit is fear. Most of us are scared to fail, scared to take a risk, and scared to leave our comfort zone. Talking becomes the wall that we lean on. Bigging-up our dreams to anyone who will listen makes us feel accomplished without actually having to do anything. Talking is safe.

But what I've discovered as I try to bag my dreams is that the more I talk about a project, the more I start to fear it. Take this book, for instance. When the idea first came to me, I just started to write toward my dream of seeing my name on the cover. But then I made the mistake of talking about it, and the fact that I was writing a book registered in my mind and

I became frighteningly nervous. I thought about the foolish statement that I had once made: *I would never be able to write a book.* And I started to believe that crap. Self-defeating thoughts rolled into an avalanche of apprehensive ones, including "No one will want to read it" and "I'm not a good enough writer." When I should have been writing, I spent precious time wallowing in unfounded fear that needed to be removed.

Then I had an epiphany. I had to stop talking. I had to stop thinking about the overwhelming task of penning a book. I had to write. I would never finish the manuscript if I didn't write. I could never be a writer if I never wrote. It's that simple.

Trash-talking doesn't just pluck nerves. It undermines our commitment ("He's not serious—he's just talking") and obstructs our ability to actually make moves. If we're really serious about pursuing our dreams, we don't need to tell others to prove it. I've gotten to the point where I hardly talk about what I'm about to do. I just let the action speak for itself.

One of my favorite questions after a person has given me the rundown of their aspirations is "What's your plan?" The second biggest hurdle in actually touching our dreams is not having a road map to get there. And that's how we get lost along the way, distracted by opportunities and pitfalls that throw us off our intended route. I used to have a sticky note on top of my computer that read, "A vision without a plan is a daydream. A plan without a vision is a nightmare." Accomplishing a goal without either a vision or a plan is like driving aimlessly without a destination in mind. You'll never get anywhere.

The last time I checked, talking has never paid the bills, nor has it catapulted someone into his or her dreams. There comes a time when all of our talk has to translate into action. Whether we aspire to change careers or change the world, stop talking about it. Plan and execute. I've stopped daydreaming. I plot, strategize, and hear the echo of Run-D.M.C. in my ear that tells me "talk is cheap."

82. Please Listen to My Demo

ARTIST: EPMD
ALBUM: UNFINISHED BUSINESS (1989)

MY **FIRST PIECE** of published writing appeared in *Black Reign News*, a Staten Island–based newspaper with a modest circulation. I spent the next few months reviewing CDs before moving on to other entertainment pieces, like movie reviews. I was writing for free, and sometimes I even had to buy the CDs! Then I got my big writing break, covering a hospital health fair in Jersey City for another local newspaper. I was paid thirty-five dollars. You couldn't tell me I wasn't on my way.

Sometimes the successful make their accomplishments seem effortless. Like they just woke up one day, and, *poof*, they controlled a multi-million-dollar company. The stories of the years spent grinding, handing out flyers, answering their own telephones, knocking on doors, or buying their own CDs to review are usually shredded like confidential documents. For this reason, many observers think they can skip the coffee-fetching flunky days and instantly take the elevator to the penthouse.

Personally, I relate to those accounts that shine a spotlight on the Grind like the one in "Please Listen to My Demo," in which EPMD reminisce about the early days before they were put on, before they became

one of hip-hop's well-known two-man crews. The track has that meditative, laid-back vibe, appropriate for storytelling. Offering hope to aspiring whatevers, Erick and Parrish recall one occasion when they were on
their way to shop their demo tape. While they fantasize about blowing up
and cashing big checks, the car overheats on the highway, and in their
"fresh" clothes Erick has to push while PMD controls the steering wheel.
That's the Grind that I know.

It would take a year for me to land another paid writing gig after the
thirty-five-dollar assignment failed to make me rich. But I kept shopping
my work to other publications. I submitted my music reviews, personal-
ity profiles, and opinion pieces to anyone who could read, in hopes that
someone would publish me. By day I was reconciling tedious promo-
tional budgets for cell phones at my full-time marketing job. By night I
was writing for my life.

Many of us are ready to roll in the Maybach but don't want to engage
in the grunt work that may be required to elevate to the top. I always
laugh when I think about *Making the Band 2* when Diddy made his aspiring protégés walk from Manhattan to Brooklyn to fetch him cheesecake.
Regardless of how I feel about Sean musically or personally, making it
requires Diddy's ride-the-train-from-Washington-DC-to-New York-to-
intern-at-Uptown type of commitment. You've got to be willing to go the
long distance.

Dream seekers also have to be fearless. Kick in doors. Be everywhere
that opportunity breathes. Pound the payment in stilettos, Tims, or
Pumas. And ask the right people to "please listen to my demo."

Ultimately you're requesting that someone give you a chance to show 'em what you got.

The first opportunity that emerges may suck. Covering that hospital health fair was as exciting as, well, writing about a hospital health fair. The initial shot of breaking through may be the chance to rock a show for free. To get a role as "Girl #6" in an independent film, or as I also did, intern in the book publishing industry to get one heel in the door. At twenty-four I was broke, living off school loans, and working for free. My boss wasn't much older than me. I, however, was embarrassingly older than the other interns, who were probably thinking about sorority initiations while I was worrying about rent. But the contacts that I gained from my stint as a glorified paper-pusher made the experience priceless.

Trying to get put on isn't for the shy, prideful, or lazy. Suck it up. Jump on it. Check your pride. Blow folks away. Live it. Breathe it. Keep the faith. Trust in your capabilities. Eventually—and it may take years—the right person will listen to your demo.

83. Spaceship

ARTIST: KANYE WEST, FEATURING CONSEQUENCE AND GLC
ALBUM: THE COLLEGE DROPOUT (2004)

EVERY DAY FOR a good year, as I trekked on a forty-five-minute subway ride to a decent-paying full-time gig that didn't make me happy, I blasted Kanye West's "Spaceship" through my iPod headphones. I was working because my finances dictated such, but I had dreams of pursuing my entrepreneurial passions. Striking out on my own sounded as crazy as going out with a complete stranger, but people do it all the time, including me. That dreadful question haunted me, *How would I make money?* Those bimonthly checks at my job weren't glamorous, but they were consistent. Consistent beats inconsistent any day. Pragmatism haunted me. I fought my heart.

I tried my best to release my frustration by listening to Kanye West and friends conceptualize how I was feeling. Who better than West to create a song about the disappointment in pursuing one's dreams? We know his story of going from Chicago rags to hip-hop riches, because he's told us on several occasions. I mostly only heard him when he did it through his music; it meant something then. Queens rapper Consequence discusses his former life where he rhymed alongside A Tribe Called Quest and how now, in his current life as he works a minuscule job, he's waiting on his spaceship to blast him back into the hip-hop game. GLC, another West colleague, brings the gangsta-who-wants-to-do-right theme.

It's West's verse that motivated me in a twisted, buck-the-system way. He's a Gap employee—and if you've ever worked retail, you feel his pain— disrespected by coworkers, but holding on to a dream in his back pocket. He spends all of his free time doing beats in the basement, eager for the Grind to pay off.

West once said in a television interview that when he developed the song, he pictured people who worked a job that they disliked, and knew there was better opportunity outside the walls of their employer. Whether it's telemarketing gigs (I know a few great MCs who make sales calls), crummy retail jobs to put yourself through school, or waitressing until your first book sells, we do what we have to until we're rescued out of monotony and into our desires.

West's spaceship blasted off, as did his head, but his success is still a worthy example of hip-hop's can't stop, won't stop drive. Waiting for our dreams to materialize doesn't mean we literally wait, twiddle our thumbs, and watch reruns of *The Sopranos*. Even when it seems like our flight is delayed indefinitely, we have to continue to prepare for takeoff.

During those subway rides to work, I plotted. When I arrived back home after a long day, spending eight-plus hours staring at a computer screen and engaging in empty small talk with other bored coworkers, I spent the rest of my evenings hustling. Preparing.

We have to trust that our passions coupled with the Grind will ignite the fire our spaceships need to blast away. Countdown approaches.

84. Rhyme Pays

ARTIST: ICE T
ALBUM: RHYME PAYS (1987)

DURING MY VALEDICTORIAN speech in high school (yes, I was a nerd and still am), I urged my fellow graduates, "Do not follow where the path may lead; go instead where there is no path, and leave a trail." I received roaring applause. But I'm sure it was because the end of my address marked us one step closer to celebratory buffets. Even though I read that quote with conviction, in retrospect I didn't really mean it.

Because after high school I embarked upon a very traditional path; not once did I consider blazing my own trail. The preset plan was quite mundane, actually. Four-year college. Bachelor's degree in business. Practical. Safe. Decent-paying job in a respectable field. Benefits. Work for the next forty years. Take some time off to pursue an advanced degree. Return to work for a bigger corporate behemoth.

After a few months of sitting in my drab gray, three-walled cubicle, I was already tired of the monotony. Bored was an understatement. My only joy was the daily trip to the cafeteria to score a vanilla cappuccino. I found myself penning poems and searching for outlets where I could write. I dreamed of starting a magazine but pushed the thought away like an annoying gnat. I wanted to pen a novel but knew that I didn't possess any formal writing training. I wanted to teach and work with books. I had occupational desires that couldn't be found in the college career center or as openings on Monster.com. Just as forerunning rappers in the '70s never imagined carving a career out of rhyming, I didn't believe it was possible for me to make money from words.

"Rhyme Pays" is a clean, rock-n-rap homage to Ice T's skills that pay the bills. In verse after verse he tells us exactly why he's in the game, but he also makes it clear that rapping not only puts food on his table but also acts as a vehicle for guys like him to leave the streets and find an alternative method of living large.

In corporate America I was far from living large. My friends were smart enough to set themselves up to be paid on the MBA, JD, and MD paths. I, with creative impulses, seemed to have only inquired a degree as an ASS.

I felt like I was hanging out with self-sabotage. So I began to seek and study the movements of passion entrepreneurs. I found that countless hip-hoppers, beyond the usual suspects of Diddy, Jay-Z, and Russell Simmons, have parlayed a passion into a career. When I came across the multifaceted career of Bobbito Garcia, I knew that it's possible to do whatever you freakin' desire.

A graduate of Wesleyan University, Robert "Bobbito" Garcia, aka DJ Cumberslice, who has as many names as he has career projects, is the epitome of hip-hop: one-half of the famous Stretch Armstrong and Bobbito hip-hop radio show; former *VIBE* magazine music columnist; cofounder of *Bounce* magazine; basketball player who had the opportunity to play professionally in his homeland, Puerto Rico; actor in films like Spike Lee's *Summer of Sam*; author of *Where'd You Get Those? New York City's Sneaker Culture: 1960–1987*; sneaker designer; music consultant; in-demand DJ; reporter for the New York Knicks; announcer for EA Sports' "NBA Street" video game; and host of ESPN2's *It's the Shoes* series. And, as he told me, his own business manager and agent. This is just a partial list. He ain't half steppin'.

When I asked Bobbito, who left a cushy job at Def Jam in 1993 and never looked back, how he managed to carve a career out of playing ball and an affinity for sneakers, words, and music, he said that it comes down to his most important credo: not being afraid to fail. Working tirelessly and being a shameless self-promoter are a close second and third. "Things aren't guaranteed," he told me. "You owe it to yourself to bust your ass."

Bobbito is unapologetic for loving a lot of things and transforming that love into a versatile career that truly represents the spirit of hip-hop culture.

Like Bobbito, I get the question all the time, "What do you do?" I also receive the strange look when my answer doesn't fit into a neat two-word title like those in my former life, such as marketing coordinator, media analyst, and marketing administrator. I'm now writer, consultant, teacher, advocate, blogger, editor, author, and looking to add more. I've got a list of goals as long as the miniseries *Roots*. Sometimes I wonder if it is all possible or if I'm even capable. Then I have to shake off the fear like excess water and charge forward.

Even O.G. Ice T veered off the rap path to start a rock band and play a detective on *Law & Order: Special Victims Unit*. Go figure, or as I like to say, go get those figures doing whatever your heart desires.

Hip-hop has illustrated that we don't have to follow a traditional path, because we can create our own. I continue to involve myself in projects that allow me to rise in the morning with a smile. We all have to do what's necessary to eat, but at the end of the day, life is shorter than sixteen bars. Shouldn't we spend our verses doing work that we love?

85. The Grind Date

ARTIST: DE LA SOUL
ALBUM: THE GRIND DATE (2004)

YOU'VE BEEN UP for at least twenty-four hours. No food. Just caffeine and sugar. Your apartment is a hot mess. You know you're tired, but you can't exactly feel it. Except in your eyes. Meeting in a few hours. Project is due. It's not done yet. But it's still due. This is your routine several nights a week. No sleep. All work.

Welcome to the Grind.

Most hip-hoppers I know operate on two channels: "Hustlemode" and "Off." "Hustlemode" is when we're courting the Grind. Doing whatever it takes to make our aspirations become reality. "Off" is usually reserved for those periods when we just shut down, take a forced vacation, or recoup some sleep—although most of us say that we'll reserve rest for the afterlife. Even in the "Off" position, we still make ourselves available, just in case someone wants to talk business. We never miss grind dates.

De La Soul has been hustling since the late '80s. And in 2004, when *The Grind Date* was released, they still hadn't stopped producing art that they believe in despite the obstacles they face in the fickle hip-hop music industry. In this De La joint, they remind us that ain't nothin' pretty in a world where the poorer get poorer and playing Xbox doesn't pay the bills. The refreshingly atypical hip-hop group put in work in the dirt, plowin' to remain relevant. Hands-on is the only way to make sure it gets done right. Step out of their way. They got a grind date to make.

Courting the Grind isn't fine wine and expensive dinners at fancy restaurants. Actually, it's rarely that. The Grind is gritty and at times grimy, showers aren't always a priority. Dating the Grind is a stream of endless phone calls, meetings, outings, and politicking. Work. Work that's masked as play. And more work. The Grind is a needy sonofahustle.

For a flash second grinders may contemplate giving up the Starbucks habit, the sleep-deprived stance, and the early-morning work sessions for an indefinite stream of quiet Netflix nights. But the thought is rushed out of our heads as quickly as we hurry friends off the phone who call us in the middle of a time-sensitive project.

Loved ones have a hard time understanding the relationship with the Grind. And I'll be the first to admit that having five simultaneous gigs isn't always suitable for balanced living, relationship-building, or dating. Some guys feel that I'm too occupied. They don't believe that I can be this busy. Nope, I tell them, I can't hang out tonight and engage in meaningless banter over cheap drinks and finger foods. Don't they know what I'm trying to do? Dig up a piece of land with my hands to build a new reality. If they can't help me plow or don't know what it's like to survive on coffee ice cream alone, I'm like Lil' Kim—I got no time. Ain't nothin' going on but my dreams.

I'll admit it, though. There is some truth to these workaholic arguments. Some of us on the Grind could play harder, work less, and carve out more time for our supporters. I've begun to seek more balance in my day-to-day and I remind myself to live, not just toil.

Truth is, if we weren't hustling to support our ambitions, many grinders would still be frontin' in jobs that make us miserable or we'd still be miles away from our aspirations. The Grind is as much about not returning to our former careers and lives as it is about crafting ones that we can be proud of.

So we attack our fields—whether we're pushing music, books, start-up businesses, or Warm Spirit products—with the vigor and force of a battering ram. The sacrifices, which range from missed parties to forfeiting time with loved ones, can be overwhelming at times. But we know inside that all of our sleepless nights, caffeine runs, and the nonstop cycle of labor will be worth the payoff of capturing our dreams.

Welcome to the Grind. Stay awhile—it's worth it.

86. Ain't No Half Steppin'

ARTIST: BIG DADDY KANE
ALBUM: LONG LIVE THE KANE (1988)

LAZINESS IS A hard beast to fight. Especially if you can half step and still get through life. Spend a day draped on the couch or handle business? Sleep or clean the house? 100 percent or 75?

Big Daddy Kane wasn't a C-average artist. In the late '80s and early '90s, the Juice Crew member constantly annihilated his competition with rhymes that were thoughtful, clever, hardworking, and mind-spinning. He was busy creating a legacy that continues to influence contemporary MCs. He was occupied with representing smoothness and Brooklyn. Oh, and he spent ample time acting as my pretend boyfriend. As a preteen, I had a collection of *Word Up!* posters of the King covering my walls, so wherever I was in the room, those lazy eyes stared back at me.

"Ain't No Half Steppin'" is a manifestation of his talent. Although he made rhyming seem effortless, there's a perfectionist quality to his art. I could picture him in front of the mic making sure every line he spit was tight as he pushed the boundaries of his creative limits (for another example check out his "Give a Demonstration"). From start to finish of the classic track, his lyrics are crisp. No trailing off, no sloppy or rushed verses. He is not coasting or reveling in mediocrity. Big Daddy Kane is giving us 100 percent.

Even in 2005, when he was honored during VH1's Hip-Hop Honors, he didn't miss one step in his performance. Kane rhymed like it was 1988. He even hit one of those dance splits that I could hardly do when I was younger and damn sure wouldn't try now. He got the job done. And took pride in doing it.

I'm trying to incorporate a Kane-type commitment in my own work. It's hella enticing to give that 75 percent and save the other quarter for a rainy day. But the risk is that we're also restricting our potential and becoming comfortable with C-level progress. Exceptional effort doesn't go unrewarded; employers to audiences will take notice. But more importantly, who doesn't love the euphoric feeling that shocks your body when you know you rocked a project, performance, or assignment? When we're tempted to half-ass it at work, in school, or during the Grind, we should think about how Kane gave it to us. No half steppin'. That's how I want to be remembered.

87. Tell Me Who Profits

ARTIST: SOULS OF MISCHIEF
ALBUM: 93 'TIL INFINITY (1993)

SHAQUILLE O'NEAL IS rich. The white man who signs Shaquille's checks is wealthy, joked Chris Rock in one of his stand-up routines.

While most of us wouldn't mind having Shaquille-type money, Rock's commentary makes you question, *Who really profits from my hard work? Am I working in vain to make a few bucks, or am I moving toward becoming the CEO signing checks?*

Rap music has turned brown kids from the block into millionaires in mansions. But it's obvious that many of them are still at the mercy of suits who won't think twice to drop them if sales/performance/quotas don't translate into a phat bottom line. It's just business, never personal. But personally, I'm interested in controlling my own business.

In "Tell Me Who Profits" California crew Souls of Mischief blast those who hustle on the block, make a little dough, but take big risks for king-pin bosses who, in the end, are the ones who really profit. The same phenomenon can be seen in the world of sports, the world of large boardrooms, the world of entertainment, and beyond.

Stacking chips is well and good, but it will only last as long as an employer allows. Whether we sing, deliver UPS packages, or toil in corporate America, we need to think about ownership of businesses and our financial futures.

I used to work for a global information firm as a media analyst, a fancy title for "telemarketer." The company collected information readily available to anyone with a telephone or access to a local library and sold it at a markup price. You've got to love America. Anyway, during my short tenure, layoff rumors were circulating like memos, so the CEO paid my department a visit to reassure us that jobs weren't going to be cut. Less than two months later, things done changed and half of our thirty-plus department was let go.

Being at the financial mercy of others is risky. The thousands of Enron employees embroiled in the company's collapse can attest to that. One minute you feel secure in your cubicle's three walls; the next minute, coffee hits the fan and your boy who works security takes away your ID badge. His response? It's just business, never personal.

It's not completely our fault that we relinquish such financial power to others. It's part of the American dream that could benefit from a total makeover: work hard at a company, get a promotion every few years, count off the days until you can receive your pension, and retire to your house with the picket fence. Unfortunately, this plan doesn't always work well for a generation that created a global culture out of desperation.

What we weren't taught, which only a few of us are now learning on our own via trial and error, is institution building and establishing financial legacies for our families, an idea that's easier in theory than in practice.

I became an independent because I wanted to justly profit from my hard labor and exert complete control over my cash flow. My energy and time is invested in growing Me, Inc. I'm no closer than the next wo(man) to achieving financial freedom and independence, and I'm just in the beginning stages of concocting a plan so that I can leave my unborn children a financial legacy. But my ears are open to the successes and mistakes of others.

I can't stop, won't stop until my money works overtime through rain, sleet, snow, and most important, when I don't feel like it. My business will always be personal.

88. Lose Yourself

ARTIST: EMINEM
ALBUM: 8 MILE: MUSIC FROM AND INSPIRED BY THE MOTION PICTURE (2002)

HAVE YOU EVER experienced a do-or-die moment? Where an oppor-tunity presented to you may be the one to change your life?

I feel like I've had a few of these "turning points," which required me to either go for mine or rip up my dreams. It was leaving Baltimore to change my life. It was moving hundreds of miles away from my comfort zone to pursue a master's degree. It was signing the contract to write this book.

Eminem's Academy Award-winning song, "Lose Yourself," musically captures the rise-and-fall plight of dream seekers. This time around, the Detroit MC's rage is projected at a perfect target: seizing your dreams. And he's knocking it out of the box. It opens with a soothing piano that quickly turns into a taunting and gritty beat with a frantic tension. There are crescendos and decrescendos. Eminem's voice inflections are just as frenetic. Then he hits you with the hook that comes like a left one to the chin. "This opportunity," he roars, "comes once in a lifetime."

Hollywood dramatized this once-in-a-lifetime moment in 8 Mile dur-ing the final battle scene. Eminem's character, Rabbit, has to either go for his or give up. If you've seen the movie, you know the melodramatic mobile-home life that awaited him.

But isn't that the reality for many of us? The anxiety we feel to achieve our dreams is fueled by the possibility of working in a dead-end job for the remainder of our days, the need to provide appropriately for our families, or the desire to emerge from a miserable existence.

When that moment, a break to prove what we've got, presents itself, everything that we've dealt with up to this point flashes in our mind.

THE HATE: You see all the faces of the people who tell you can't do it. The voices become louder. They taunt you because you're from the wrong side of town. You're the wrong color. The wrong sex. You're fooling yourself.

THE SACRIFICES: You planned, plotted, and strategized. You kept your eyes on the prize and off everything else. You neglected other aspects of your life. You prayed, hoped, and wished. You did whatever it took. You left home. You left your children. You slept on a friend's couch. You held down two jobs to pay for what your dream couldn't.

THE ANXIETY: How much more can you handle? How much longer can you work without seeing that light at the end of the tunnel? You've got to change your situation. It's now or never. Got to get out of your neighborhood. Rent is due. Ends aren't meeting.

THE REJECTION: You were told you can't do it. You were declined. You were fired. You were booed. Not good enough. "Sorry, but you're not what we're looking for right now."

THE SELF-DOUBT: Indecision. Fear. The thoughts begin to circle in your head. Who are you to pursue this dream? You're really not that good. Everyone is right, you should give up.

PERFORMANCE TIME: Do you choke? Do you deliver? Do you follow through? Do you embrace the challenge? This is your chance. There are no options.

At this point you know what you have to do. You have to go for it. Deep breath. Exhale. Give 100 percent. Lose yourself.

But what then, if you mess up, tomato-throwing–style? It happens. And this is why I don't subscribe to the idea that there is only one opportunity that will transport us to where we want to be, and if for some reason we aren't successful at it, our dream is forever cut short. The point is to treat every opportunity like it's the only one. To maintain the mind-set that you are going to give it all you've got. Many of us mistakenly take opportunity too lightly, in that nonchalant, oh-there-will-be-another-chance way. So, we opt to do nothing when a big break slaps us in the face. We don't seize. We let it pass. Subsequently, we are kept in our dire situations, and we are doing the keeping.

Within our muddy lives of bills, responsibilities, and drama, opportunity still exists. But can we notice it? And if we do see it, do we attack it?

Maybe a big break hasn't presented itself. Be ready. In the meantime, throw on Eminem's motivational workout. Blast it. Scream the hook. Feel the energy. Arm yourself with the power to seize. Lose yourself in opportunity.

89. Ready or Not

ARTIST: FUGEES
ALBUM: THE SCORE (1996)

ONE OF MY favorite childhood games was hide-and-seek. After counting to twenty, I would proudly announce, "Ready or not, here I come." What I loved about this simple activity is that although there's that waiting period, which seemed like an eternity as a youngster, when time is up you don't ask for permission to go seeking. Whether your opponents were ready or not, you were coming.

The first time I heard the Fugees, the innovative trio from New Jersey, was on their mishap called "Boof Baf," an unfortunate cut from their 1994 debut album, *Blunted on Reality*. The song made me foreshadow their future as fixtures in the $2.99 bin at the local music store. Perhaps I just wasn't ready for them.

Nonetheless, the group went back to the lab, reengineered their sound, repositioned themselves, and reemerged with vengeance. The result, *The Score*, a heavy rotator in my collection, sold a disgusting number of copies. One of the hottest tracks from the album is "Ready or Not," which features one of the meanest Lauryn Hill verses of all time (she steals the spotlight from her partners once again), where she knocks Al Capone imitators by conjuring up the spirit of Nina Simone. Ms. Hill makes it look easy.

But it is truly the song's hook that is the motivational kicker, part of the declaration call from hide-and-seek, where ready or not, the Fugees were coming with a style and vibe that we couldn't hide from. The world was ready this time around. Eager, hungry even, for accessible sociopolitical rap from a group with an exceptional female MC. Who would have guessed?

Years after my hide-and-seek days, I find myself announcing, in a voice that reflects maturity and experience, not to childhood play buddies, but this time to the world, that "ready or not, here I come." I'm coming with words from the heart. I'm coming with intellect and creativity. I'm coming with my hip-hop self. Ready. Or. Not.

As I've prepared for my emergence, it's apparent that people aren't always going to be ready for what you have to offer, whether it's your talent, intellect, love, or persona. You may have to play Thomas Edison and show them the light (bulb). Or you may have to accept the fact that they may never be ready. Luckily, that's their problem, not yours. Can't waste time waiting on the nonbelievers or the slow ones; it will interrupt your mission to take over the world and disrupt the daily job of doing you.

On the flip side, how many times have you heard, "Heads ain't ready, son"? We sometimes say this or some variation, because in fact we are the ones who are stalling. More often than not it has nothing to do with timing; there's usually a mixture of unaddressed anxiety, uncertainty, and fear chilling in the background. This type of noise is far more damaging than that provided by nonbelievers. The sound can be deafening.

So silence the inner noise and the outer chatter, and listen to your heart's voice. After it speaks, make the announcement, "Ready or not, here I come," and then bring it.

90. Crossover

ARTIST: EPMD
ALBUM: BUSINESS NEVER PERSONAL (1992)

DURING ONE OF my lazy afternoons hanging out online at YouTube, I saw an old Jaz video that featured a very young, awkward, and skinny Shawn Carter. I almost didn't recognize Jay-Z rapping alongside his former mentor. Besides being several years younger and pounds lighter, to my surprise, the self-proclaimed one-man business was rocking an African medallion. Jay-Z the hustler? An African medallion?

That's when I thought about his eye-opening rhyme from his first retirement disc, *The Black Album*. In "Moment of Clarity" Jay-Z spits that he wants to rap like multidimensional Common, who is known for his complex and socially aware lyrics, but after selling five million records, he hasn't rhymed like Common since. In that clever swagger-filled way only Jay-Z can muster, he admits that he's a sellout. I can't knock the hustle. And I damn sure appreciate his honesty.

Although you wouldn't guess it from the current bling state of main-stream hip-hop music, one of the culture's cardinal sins is selling out: consciously crafting music that will pop or that has mass appeal in efforts to line your pockets. You're supposed to keep it real, son.

Here's the tricky part: everyone, including this writer, wants to get paid. So how do we do avoid sellout status and live comfortably?

EPMD's "Crossover" is an entry in the hip-hop rule book (after A Tribe Called Quest's industry rule #4080) about selling out. With a recognizable Roger Troutman sound, the song has this "yes'm" menacing hook that begins "whatever you want." Erick and Parrish verbally stomp on rappers who throw on suits, drop their "rough, rugged, and raw" mentality, top R&B charts, and return to the hood whitewashed.

Is this why Jay-Z, the multimillion-dollar brand, and Def Jam President/CEO feels like a "Black Republican"?

Back in the day, your Hammers and Vanilla Ices were easy sell-out targets. Pinpointing one now is a little more complicated. Is it posing in Gap commercials like Common? Rapper Styles P accused 50 Cent of being too removed from the streets. What did we expect from a rapper who named his album the by-any-means-necessary proclamation *Get Rich or Die Tryin'*? Some members of academia think author, media darling, and professor Michael Eric Dyson is too mainstream because he's constantly on television and pumps out books that people without multiple degrees want to read. Is he a sellout, too?

While these examples show how thorny the definition of "sellout" has become, they thankfully have nothing to do with you or me. The concept of "selling out" is an individual issue. For me, there's a thin line between idealism and starvation. Between that loan shark Sallie Mae and my own plastic panacea called credit cards, I've got bills, bills, bills. I embrace the ability to pay my rent and have dough left over for a sunny day in Soho. Is it a crime that I don't want to eat tuna from a can for the rest of my life?

In listening to "Crossover" and pulling back the heavy drapes of "realness," it becomes clear that being able to afford trips abroad, multiple-course dinners, and a few residential properties cannot be what drives me to write. It may drive me to work hard, but the moment that these materialistic desires start to dictate my art, that's when I will be a sellout. That is the moment that I'm no longer true to myself or my talent. That's the moment when I'm no longer real.

Selling out isn't about how many promotions we get, whether or not we trade in the jersey for a suit, what college we attended, or how many records we sell, it's about whether or not we compromise our personal ideals and beliefs to do it. Because no matter how large we get, I'll guarantee there's going to be some hater calling us a sellout merely based on our level of achievement. As individuals, it's up to us to decide how far we're willing to go and what we're willing to do to be successful. Are you willing to downplay your ethnicity to climb the corporate ladder? Are you willing to create subpar art that you know will sell? How much are you willing to play the game, and at what point will you walk away when you're no longer feeling the rules?

Call me idealistic, but I think you can remain true to yourself and still get that money. It's about finding a balance that you're comfortable with, one that respects your convictions.

Yes, I'm interested in writing for my life, achieving both critical and commercial success. But if I have to sacrifice my art, my ideals, or my person for a check, you can shuck that jive. C.R.E.A.M. (Cash Rules Everything Around Me) isn't the only indicator of accomplishment. True personal success is freedom.

Erick and Parrish aren't the only ones who aspire to make dollars. And trust, Jay-Z ain't the only one who wants to rap like Common.

91. Mo Money Mo Problems

ARTIST: THE NOTORIOUS B.I.G., FEATURING PUFF DADDY AND MASE
ALBUM: LIFE AFTER DEATH (1997)

I N 2006 PRINCETON University researchers conducted a study to gauge the connection between money and happiness. While most of us believe if we had more money, we would be more content and satisfied with our lives, the study's findings regarding the impact of income on "subjective well-being" contradicted that belief. Simply put, money may not buy our happiness.

The Notorious B.I.G. wasn't around for the results of this study. But he already concluded that contrary to what many of us think—that money is our life's savior—the truth is that the more money you acquire, the more problems arise.

"Mo Money Mo Problems" is one of my least favorite Biggie hits. Although I love the original Diana Ross song "I'm Coming Out," from which it was sampled, for this Notorious B.I.G fan, I found his version watered down. What I do appreciate about the song is its sentiment, which, coming from the self-dubbed Black Frank White—an ex-drug dealer who once said that he struggled to feed his daughter—is pretty powerful.

I don't suffer from "mo money, mo problems." It's more like *no* money, mo problems. How am I going to pay my rent this month? We've all been there, when the needs outweigh the bank account. Money can do lots of things: keep you out of jail; afford you the latest, greatest whatever; buy you a pretty arm piece, but it will not eradicate all of life's problems. It may just exacerbate them.

For the basis of a documentary titled *Reversal of Fortune*, a homeless man was given one hundred thousand dollars in cash as a social experiment to see how the money would change his life. The clips from the documentary that I viewed on *The Oprah Winfrey Show* followed forty-five year old Ted Rodrigue, as he bought a truck that cost more than thirty thousand dollars, purchased gifts for people, and acted incredibly generous. In the end he was left penniless and said that the experience confirmed his negative thoughts about people, many of whom came along when he had some dough and immediately rolled out when he didn't. Money changed his life for the worst.

I have a friend who jokes that now that he has dough he has fewer problems. And I'm sure there are many rich folks out there who would cosign that theory. Part of me agrees, but part of me knows that when we get more money, we not only enter a new tax bracket, we also upgrade our lifestyle, acquire more bills and debt, and usher in new responsibilities.

Money begins to complicate our lives. We embark on the continuous chase of it. Greed invades us like U.S. military forces and clouds our judgment. We find ourselves making ill-advised moves just to get a check.

Who can go back to Top Ramen noodles after foie gras? We go down the path toward selling our soul to the highest bidder on eBay.

Some of us use our new money to buy emotional connections to people who previously wouldn't smile in our direction. Then paranoia hits. Who can we trust? Our family and friends turn a shady color of green.

See? Complicated, right? And I'm just writing this from observation, not experience. I'm a simple girl. Yeah, I have an affinity for exotic trips and fine threads, but at what cost?

Many of our hip-hoppers, from rappers to basketball players, weren't ready to become millionaires, and the results weren't always rosy; there have been a nice number of folks filing for Chapter II. Hip-hop tells us to get that money, but then doesn't tell us productive things to do with it. Does Jacob the Jeweler sell financial freedom? Dealing with money takes a certain type of maturity, self-control, and knowledge.

Don't get it twisted. I'm on a mission to be comfortable. I have aspirations that only money can settle, like paying back that chick Sallie Mae. I am working on a path, albeit a slow one, to financial freedom and being able to splurge when I want. But I heed Biggie's warning. I don't need mo problems in my life.

92. *Vapors*

ARTIST: BIZ MARKIE
FROM: GOIN' OFF (1988)

THERE'S A SERIOUS disease affecting thousands of people. To see a microcosm of this epidemic, visit any nightclub and spend time in its VIP section. It is here, beyond the velvet ropes or in a secretly enclosed room, that you will see vaporized individuals. These victims are over-powered by the Big Three—money, power, and respect—and cling to fig-ures they perceive have the (juice) champagne. To understand the disease more, let us examine the primary text.

In "Vapors" Biz Markie presents typical scenarios in which folks have caught the sickness. An instructional video also accompanies the song, which primarily takes place on a yacht and features members of Biz's crew who have come into contact with vaporized individuals. You may have observed many of these situations before. There's the money-hungry chick who wouldn't give you the time of day because you didn't have enough zeroes in your bank account. But now that you're making some dough, she kicks out full contact information. Or there's the situa-tion that smooth operator Big Daddy Kane apparently experienced, where everyone seemed to disrespect him, declared that he'd never succeed, but when he proved them wrong, their hands were extended for more than handshakes. And the following example has happened to me: You look for a job or an opportunity, and everyone seems to tell you "no," so you find a way to make it on your own. The same folks who told you "no" want to offer you bonuses to "join the team." Typical. Biz ends the rhyme with a personal story about how he tried to get down with various DJing crews but was treated like a "wet food stamp." Ouch. He went from paying to enter parties to being the main attraction. Everyone who stood in his way was quick to step aside and ask for a ride on his coattails.

Vaporized individuals only want to get up on it—the "it" being success, money, prestige—when it's hot but don't want anything to do with you when you're traveling to get to it. Like Momma, they want a call when you've arrived.

Although I am not close to blowing up, I like to think my pilot light is on. As I've pulled out weeds along my path to success, I've come across people who are slow to realize my potential. They're skeptical for unknown reasons, and while I may invest some energy in convincing them of my ability, it's ultimately their decision. Since I am a lover of maintaining lists, I make a mental note of what they choose. Currently there are about five or six people on the "Missed the Yacht" list. I'm not interested in seeking cold-dished revenge, but their nonbelieving behavior is a clear symptom of vaporization, which I will keep in mind should I blow up like balloons at a birthday party.

I stay away from people with the vapors in their eyes—an intense green color that brightens when they come into contact with any of the Big Three—whether they're in VIP or at a family barbeque. And I stick with the folks who've been here for me when I was unemployed and hungry. The "Down from Day One" list.

93. *Ether*

ARTIST: NAS

ALBUM: STILLMATIC (2001)

I **WAS A** sensitive child. Cry at the drop of an insult. Cry at the drop of a bad grade. Cry if I didn't make a home run in kickball. I didn't allow myself to make mistakes, to be human. In efforts to curb my vulnerability, when I was about seven, my father sat me down for one of those parental talks that was more like a pep talk with a coach. He reenacted examples from great sports legends who had a bad game (most of which went over my girly head, but I think he mentioned something about Michael Jordan being cut from his high school basketball team), and I got the lesson. We all fall down. But the greatest pick themselves up.

Although Nas is one of the best to ever bless a mic, he isn't immune to falling off either. Remember "You Owe Me," that dreadful, unoriginal collaboration with R&B crooner Ginuwine? I know I wasn't the only one to wonder, *WTF? Nas, what's going on?* With *Illmatic* set as his bar, every project he does is judged against this stellar achievement.

And this is what we do. We don't allow our talented to make mistakes. We burn them at the stake if they don't always perform at an *Illmatic* level.

The pressure.

But Nas didn't doubt his lyrical prowess when he recorded his Jay-Z beef song, "Ether." The title, which by no coincidence, is defined as both a colorless, volatile, highly flammable liquid and the fifth and highest element after air, earth, fire, and water. Nas had to counter haters, skeptical fans, including this writer, and any internal uncertainty to confront Jay-Z, the proclaimed King of New York. Again, the pressure.

So Nas did what he does best: dropped one of the meanest rhymes in recent hip-hop history. When it was first released, my homeboy and I listened to it repeatedly, and I swear each time it gave me chills. "Ether" reclaimed Nas's lyrical crown, and fans forgot about those lackluster projects. The word even took on a new definition: to *etherize* means to obliterate the competition. With true hip-hop swagger, he reminded us that his lyrics were still sick and, if necessary, he can demolish any challenge just as quickly, with *Illmatic* calmness and confidence. Shut this fan up.

In my adult life the sensitivity I experienced as a child has transformed into an immense pressure that I put on myself to always bring my "A" game. As a writer, I constantly worry about the quality of my work. Artists can cosign that creative expression is one of the hardest and most gut-wrenching professions. You're regularly questioning your skills and your decision to pursue such a thorny path. I've spent countless hours in front of the computer when the words don't form or come together, feeling the sharp end of writer's block. The sentences that do emerge are garbage. Self-doubt sets in: *Do I really got it like that? Or have I been fooling myself into thinking that I can do this?*

To say that we aren't perfect is to state the obvious. But if you're like me, a self-induced perfectionist who is far from perfect, we should allow our imperfections to grant us the occasional pass for leaving our "A" game at home. This doesn't mean that we are less than great, or that we've lost that Michael Jordan touch.

This is what I know: greatness isn't a vaccine for wackness. Every project that we do isn't going to be flawless. In fact, there may be times when what we do is straight trash. Or like Pops would say, we may miss the winning shot and blow the championship. It sucks.

We may all fall off at some point, but it's the ability to come back from a failed project, bad career move, or off day that separates the greatest from everyone else.

True talent is like energy—it can't be destroyed.

94. Proceed

ARTIST: THE ROOTS
FROM: DO YOU WANT MORE?!!!??! (1995)

THERE ARE DAYS when I wake up and I'm tempted to disown this writing career, get a job, and coast. There are days when I wake up so tired of all the primetime drama called My Life that it's as if I didn't sleep at all. There are days when I crave an indefinite commercial break where all I'm required to do is breathe.

"Proceed" is a subtle motivational song without the hype. In one word the Roots capture the solution to my desire to quit. Over the group's mellow-my-man sound, Black Thought and Malik B. discuss their musical journey. Black Thought rhymes that he received his record contract in 1993, and more than a decade later, even when he feels like blinking himself away, he continues to "rock the mic."

I like that word, *proceed*. It has its own internal drill sergeant. It implies forward movement. A journey where you don't look back. Progression and continuity. Proceed. I like that word.

But even as I consider divorcing this writing life, I know I wouldn't be happy. I truly only feel complete in it. This writing life is like my husband; it may pluck my nerves, may exacerbate situations, but I love it no matter what. I'm committed. I take my vows seriously. Hypothetically speaking, if I were to leave this life behind, where would I reside? I didn't like the interior design of corporate America. Bottom line: I would be lost. We have our rough patches, but with patience and strength we'll make it through.

Change, drama, and weariness are all inevitable, but survival of the fittest is as much about perseverance as it is about one's ability to compete. My writing life and I resemble an old married couple. We do that keep on keepin' on dance where we shuffle forward with both feet. We proceed.

Along the way, the hope is that you smarten up, become wiser to the journey. With each day, I learn more about my writing life. Its likes, dislikes, temperaments. I try to be flexible and understanding. Just as a partner should.

On those days when I wake up feeling tempted to stop the journey, I blink a few times to visualize the bright future ahead of me and my partner and proceed to my computer to begin again. I wrote and illustrated my first book at age five in 1984, so I've known my partner for more than twenty years. We continue to build upon that foundation.

Proceed. I like that word.

95. The Whole World Lookin' at Me

ARTIST: BUSTA RHYMES
ALBUM: WHEN DISASTER STRIKES (1997)

WHEN I—A college graduate, daughter, sister, and friend with potential—left Baltimore "to become somebody," I knew that I would not only have to fulfill the unknown destiny that I envisioned for myself but I would also have to accomplish the aspirations that my world—family, friends, lovers, colleagues—had for me. I was propelled to star in my life's play, *Black Girl Dreams.*

Ambition is both a blessing and a curse. I sympathize with those who don't have it, and I feel for those who do. The ambitionless aren't consumed with an internal and external pressure to be successful. The ambitious aren't only consumed, but we also feel like the entire world is patiently and impatiently waiting for us to achieve heights of distinction. I can hear the clock ticking as I write this. The audience is waiting for my show. Ambition and pressure are a package deal.

On his second solo album, where the stakes are higher, Busta Rhymes dedicated a song to this reality. In "The Whole World Lookin' at Me" he doesn't stumble or falter at the fact that he's under pressure; instead he soaks up the energy, transforms it into positive vibes, and rhymes like his life depends on it. And it does.

Busta becomes a ghetto guru as he shouts throughout the song, "I feel so supreme." And to calm my nerves before I get on stage to star in *Black Girl Dreams*, I repeat after him, "I feel so supreme."

For the ambitious, there's the internal tension to prove to our worlds that we didn't make a mistake quitting our job, moving miles away, or switching careers to capture our dreams. When I return to Baltimore from taking over the world, I want to have a piece of it with me as evidence.

There's also the external pressure to challenge stereotypes and environmental mandates that dictate how far we are supposed to go before we have a chance to read the travel directions.

Ambition and pressure are a package deal. I don't want to forget my lines when I'm front and center on stage.

Let's not be presumptuous. What's scarier than everyone waiting on us is that no one will care. Empty seats at the debut of our dreams. Complete and utter silence. Writers like to say that we write for ourselves. That's partly true. We also write with the hope that an audience, beyond Momma and them, will take pleasure in our words. If I didn't want to be read, I would keep a diary with one of those small combination locks.

The ambitious spend a great deal of time preparing for the role of a lifetime, the one that will illuminate our brilliance. We spend countless hours practicing our skill, performing for smaller audiences. But most importantly, we have to learn the art of transforming pressure into positive energy so that on opening night, when the whole world is lookin' at us, everyone will be blown away. Encore?

96. Move the Crowd

ARTIST: ERIC B. & RAKIM
ALBUM: PAID IN FULL (1987)

THERE'S NOTHING BETTER than seeing your favorite group perform live and rip it. There's nothing worse than seeing a group live who make you wish you were at home watching one of their videos instead. A few years ago I was pumped to see a beloved hip-hop team do their thing in Jersey. They didn't do their thing. I'm not quite sure what they were doing. There was no energy. No enthusiasm. No crowd participation. It was like the three of them were having a private cipher in their basement. They didn't even pull out the foolproof "wave your hands in the air" when things got really bad. The group didn't have a plan. They should have listened to "Move the Crowd."

Rakim provides performers, not just rappers, with a blueprint for rocking an audience. Check it: he's chilling at a party, by the speakers, feeling the music flow through his veins when he catches the itch to get on stage and rock it. But first he's got to figure out how he's going to "move the crowd." Rakim's approach becomes a mix of perfection, where no mistakes are allowed; chemistry, where he and Eric B. vibe; surprise, where he blesses the audience with special effects; and spirituality, where Allah rhymes through him. As always, he throws in dashes of that Rakim cool to command the room.

Although we may not think of ourselves as entertainers (like we're on stage at the Apollo singing the first verse of "His Eye Is on the Sparrow" before the fickle crowd boos us), we are actually constantly performing at work, in school, and in life.

Before I give a workshop, speak in front of an audience group, or meet with potential clients, I have to devise a game plan to connect with my audience. Likewise, anytime I write something, anything, I have to think about how I'm going to engage readers so that they feel my words.

The art of performance isn't only about having good content; it's also about making the audience believe in you. It's what Kool Herc did when he studied the crowd and realized that the partygoers would spend their time dancing on the song's break. He gained their respect. It's what Afrika Bambaataa implied on "Looking for the Perfect Beat" to find the precise medium to unite with his listeners.

I still clapped for my beloved hip-hop group as they exited the stage after their lackluster performance. The goal is always to leave the audience satisfied but craving more. Unfortunately, they made me feel like I had heard more than enough. It's not easy to connect with an audience. To make them turn the page. To make them request your work again. To make them give you a standing ovation. But before stepping on stage, those cats should have asked themselves Rakim's poignant question, "How could I move the crowd?"

97. The Formula

ARTIST: THE D.O.C.
ALBUM: NO ONE CAN DO IT BETTER (1989)

IF SUCCESS WERE packaged and sold, what would the ingredients be? How much should it cost? How much would you be willing to pay? Even though I know Success in a Bottle™ would be a best seller, I have no aspirations to hawk such a product. I wouldn't feel right selling hope when in fact the keys to success are right before our eyes, available to anyone for free.

My sister and I used to repeatedly blast The D.O.C.'s album *No One Can Do It Better* from her tape player. The solo debut from former N.W.A. crew member is funky, fresh, and dope, minus the intense gangsterism. With Dr. Dre on the track, "The Formula" proves the D.O.C.'s artistic prowess. In a mellow, but hard-hitting tone, he reveals the secrets to his lyrical dexterity: knowledge and talent. But in fact, if you sit down with "The Formula" and analyze it as hip-hoppers do, you realize that the entire composition is a lyrical blueprint for greatness, the recipe for Success in a Bottle™.

Below is what Chef D.O.C. recommends. I have some of the ingredients and am working on acquiring the others.

ENERGY: Have lots of it. You'll need it for the longevity of your plight.

WISDOM: The D.O.C. mentions this at the beginning of his first verse, so it's crucial.

KNOWLEDGE: This is one of the most important ingredients. Have plenty of it.

COMMON SENSE: Be practical, but also establish the mentality of the successful.

STYLE OR UNIQUENESS: Establish a personal and well-defined style.

INTERPERSONAL SKILLS: Know how to have healthy and effective interaction with others.

CREATIVITY AND INNOVATION: Distinguish yourself from the competition.

COMPETITIVE: Strive to be better than your competitors.

TALENT: Make sure you're tapping into the depth of your gifts.

ORIGINALITY: Develop innovative ways of presenting yourself.

WINNING SPIRIT: Think and act like a winner.

PROGRESSION: Look to move forward and become better as you grow.

PREPARATION: Devote time to your skill.

PATIENCE: Timing is important; don't rush unnecessarily.

CONFIDENCE: Know that you have what it takes to be great, and you'll convince others.

There you have it, the recipe for Success in a Bottle™ laced in the lyrics of a hip-hop song. None of the ingredients are unobtainable. Success is in our reach if we are willing to put in the prep time.

98. *Paid in Full*

ARTIST: ERIC B. & RAKIM
ALBUM: PAID IN FULL (1987)

HAVE YOU EVER been broke? You know insufficient-funds broke, where you don't have enough money in your bank account to make a minimum withdrawal from the ATM? Or you check your pockets and you can't pull together enough lint to buy a subway ride?

Rakim knows what I'm talking about. "Paid in Full" is both a testament to being broke and a plan for overcoming it. He begins by defining how penniless he is. In this case, he's sweaty-palmed broke. Still, he does the mandatory checking of the pockets for verification. Now he's strategizing. How can he make some dough? He embarks upon a moment of truth. He could revert to his old days of being a stick-up kid to make some cash, but he's found Allah and rolls righteously. Robbing for a quick buck is no longer an option. He brushes the thought off and sees a ray of sunshine in his relatively dark situation. He even starts to whistle. The thought of pursuing a nine-to-five hits him as a viable possibility, but his passion, rhyming, nags him. He's tired of fantasizing about living comfortably. So he goes in the direction of the studio to turn his talent into income. His master plan begins to come together.

What's so great about this single-verse song is that the first line encapsulates one of the keys for prosperity. Rakim says simply, "thinking of a master plan." And this is where we should begin.

For a long time I just wanted to write. It was cool for a while to see my byline in publications that I read, but my financial ambitions were bigger. I needed to be more systematic about how I approached my career. I needed to have a plan.

So I got one. Whipped out my laptop, pulled up a blank Word document and constructed a strategy. And although aspects of my master plan may change, the fact that it is down on paper keeps me focused on the big picture: making a healthy living from my words.

Rakim once told journalist Brian Coleman that the name of this song came from the original check that he and partner Eric B. received from their first record deal. It read: "Paid in Full." Think about your master plan and execute it. Who wants to be "paid partially," "paid insufficiently," or "paid a little"?

99. Marathon

ARTIST: DILATED PEOPLES
ALBUM: NEIGHBORHOOD WATCH (2004)

WHEN I WAS in better shape and younger, I used to run cross-country. The switch to long-distance running from the sprinting that I enjoyed and excelled at as a preteen was difficult and, thus, didn't last long. On Sundays, while my competitors in these weekly, lengthy races steadily jogged the entire haul, I found myself walking one-third of the way through. Tired. Out of breath. Ready for a car to come pick me up. I joined up with another "quitter" who was just as slow as myself. She and I would reach the finish line, and only our parents would be left waiting for us. We'd stroll through, socializing, resigned in the fact that cross-country wasn't our cup of Gatorade.

In "Marathon" Dilated Peoples, the Cali-based trio, turn into lyrical coaches and offer training advice for the long distance of life. As a group that has been around since the '90s, they're more than qualified to provide advice on preparing for the marathon versus the sprint.

I have a couple of buddies who have run marathons. I'm always amazed at their dedication, thinking in the back of my head it's something I could never do. Twenty-six freakin' miles? Those who've already completed a marathon tell me I can do it. Anyone, they say, can do it. To me, the very thought of running a distance equivalent to going from the east side of Baltimore over to the west side sounds absurd.

But they who've run a marathon, and who aren't professional runners, are right. That's the beauty of the mind, the beauty of preparation, the beauty of a plan. With training, patience, a clear mind, and hard work, anyone—including this out-of-shape chick who becomes tired when she even thinks about exerting significant physical energy—can complete one.

Then I also realize that I've run several marathons already. I might not have had on those cute shorts and matching pair of New Balance shoes to run through the streets of New York in the city's annual competition, but this sista has finished plenty of races. Slow and steady.

You can't tell me this book wasn't a marathon. You can't tell me that grad school wasn't a marathon. You can't tell me surviving Boston for two years as a single black woman wasn't a marathon! You can't tell me grinding in New York and paying sky-high rent isn't a marathon. You can't tell me I haven't been running my entire life. To opportunity. Around obstacles and past fear. Toward my destiny. Like Dilated Peoples assert, we shouldn't run from a challenge—we should "run to it."

We're all runners. Life is just one looped marathon. This is not a sprint. We have to pace ourselves. Slow and steady. Unshakeable dedication. Consistent training. Run with calculation. And retain the mind-set of a champion: the marathon isn't over until we reach the finish line.

100. The Symphony

ARTIST: MARLEY MARL, FEATURING MASTA ACE, CRAIG G, KOOL G RAP, BIG DADDY KANE
ALBUM: IN CONTROL, VOL. 1 (1988)

WHEN WE HEAR the word "symphony," we usually envision white men wearing blond wigs, who spend years composing classical masterpieces. And when the opus is finally released to the world, it blesses the masses with brilliance for generations to come.

When you mention "The Symphony" to hip-hop heads, the first thing that comes to mind isn't much different, except that instead of white men wearing blond wigs, we visualize members of the Juice Crew, black men in front of a studio mic, spitting rhymes. And since "The Symphony" was released to the world in the late '80s, it, too, continues to bless the masses with its brilliance.

"The Symphony" beams of a golden era in hip-hop and remains a blueprint for the posse hit. It's one of the most recognizable tracks in our culture's history, and to rock on it, the MCs—Masta Ace, Craig G, Kool G Rap, and Big Daddy Kane—had to make sure that their rhymes were funky. I wonder if they knew then that what they were creating was a masterpiece. It's got to be a supreme feeling to be forever associated with a song as influential.

That got me thinking, *How will I be remembered? What will be my life's symphony? How will I leave my mark on the world?*

Masterpieces are usually a quintessential piece of work that defines one's career. Lauryn Hill's *The Miseducation of Lauryn Hill*. Ralph Ellison's *Invisible Man*. Alice Walker's *The Color Purple*. I would be honored to create a work on the level of any of these artistic creations, but I don't want to get trapped trying to pen the sweeping novel. Some of us are looking to craft that singular work of genius but get so caught up in the process that we generate nothing.

So I look at all that I do—my writing, my literacy initiatives, helping others—as contributing to my symphony's composition. I want to shape a legacy that will leave a collective impression on many. As an educator for more than thirty years, my mother's masterpiece is the thousands of children she's helped, a gift that will continue to benefit the world even when she retires. How do *you* want to be remembered?

I'm vested in making everything that I release, touch, or get involved in a heart-plus-soul production. I want to leave value behind. So that one day, when my entire head is gray, I'm sporting a pink housecoat, sitting in a big, wooden rocking chair on a country porch with my grandchildren in my lap, and telling stories of the "good ole days," I can proudly say, "Yes, Grandmomma did that."